Mrs Geo. B. Jett
6 2 N. Reese

If You Live With Little Children

If You
Live
With
Little Children

by
Carolyn Kauffman
and
Patricia Farrell

Illustrated by Al Zelver
and Carmen Gilbert

G. P. Putnam's Sons   New York

For

Herby
Al
Nicky
Mike
David
Jimmy
Elizabeth
May and
Kay

For in their [parents'] uneasiness as to how to bring up their children they turn increasingly to books, magazines, government pamphlets, and radio programs. These tell the already anxious mother to accept her children. She learns to look into her own pysche whenever she is moved to deny the children anything, including an uninterrupted flow of affection. If the children are cross then the mother must be withholding something. And while these tutors also tell the mother to "relax" and to "enjoy her children," even this becomes an additional injunction to be anxiously followed.

—The Lonely Crowd
David Riesman

PREFACE

This book is a collection of ideas for having fun with preschool children. It is during these first five years that parents have their main opportunity to know and play with their children. Yet these years are often filled with so much confusion, so much "getting through" the daily routine, that this opportunity just to have a good time together can be lost. When our children start school the problems change, and an interesting, delightful age has slipped by.

We believed that if parents had the time—which they certainly do not—to have a cup of coffee with lots of different parents, they would probably pick up tips that would make life easier and more enjoyable. So this is how we did the research for our book. We talked and sent questionnaires to all our friends, and friends of friends, who, simply by living with little children, have learned many useful "tricks of the trade."

Some of the ideas are old ones that will be new to many of you. Some of the ideas are brand-new. And none of them depend on much money, special equipment or even special talents.

We do not expect, nor even suggest, that you use all of these ideas. But we think it is a book you might open in the evening, after a day that did not seem to go quite right, and discover a suggestion that will give you a needed pickup, a fresh start, for the next day.

Besides this, we have included ideas for special events, such as Halloween costumes you can make, recipes for preschool cooks, ways to entertain a sick child, and many others.

We are not child pyschologists, and are not advising you how to raise your children. Instead, we have filled the book with different ways to enjoy them.

One of us has taught in a nursery school for many years. The other has published a number of children's stories.

But we think our most important "credential" is that we both live with little children, too.

TABLE OF CONTENTS

If You Live With Little Children

PLEASE, WON'T YOU PLAY
OUTDOORS ?

To dig and delve in nice clean dirt
Can do a mortal little hurt.

J. Bangs

<u>Setting</u>

Something to dig in, something to swing on, something to splash in, something to climb on, something to ride on, something to jump on, something to walk on, something to sit on, something to lie down on, something to push, something for creeping and crawling.

OUTDOOR PLAY EQUIPMENT

Not all people have the same space available for play, and in some cases it may be very limited. Among the suggestions here you will be able to find many that are not dependent upon a large play area.

SOMETHING TO DIG IN

<u>Sand is Grand.</u>

Sandboxes can be any shape or size.

A free form made of concrete can be a wading pool too, if you add a drain.

A sand dune in the corner of the back yard is good enough.

A box 6' x 6' is standard.

Sand toys:
    Wooden spoons and bowls
    Strainers
    Colanders
    Funnels
    Old pans
    Scoops
    Toy cars and trucks

Sand molds:
    Measuring cups
    Plastic glasses
    Plastic or aluminum bowls
    Muffin tins
    Jello molds

Children like wet sand. It makes castles taller. Some children like their sand really wet. It's a good idea to turn the hose off after filling a few buckets and pans with water.

Cats like sand too. Here are some ways to change their minds:
1. Lay a tarpaulin or boards across the sand at night.
2. A screen in a wooden frame is light and easy to manage.

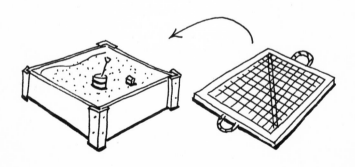

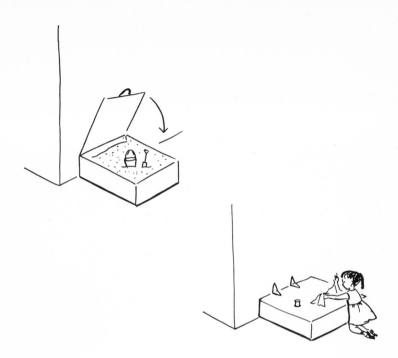

3. A cover that hooks to the side of a garage becomes a worktable when it is down.

   Children who sit in sandboxes need shade.
1. The eaves of a house or the shade of a tree is a natural setting.
2. A canopy can be made from canvas.

3. A 6' x 6' bamboo shade provides a filtered light.

And something to sit on.

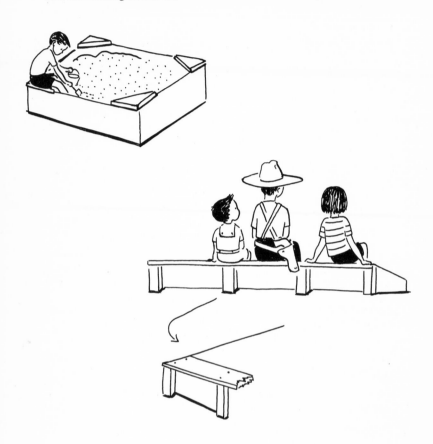

Sand rules:

No fair throwing.
Brush yourself off before you come in the house.
Keep the sand in the sandbox.
Ask permission to play with water on account of colds.
No sterling silver in the sandbox.

Dirt and Mud

Two hills of hard-packed dirt make a good place to play Cowboy and Indian, Can't Catch a Nanny Goat, and games of that nature.

Dirt and water   Mud is a summer
make mud.   activity.

If you do not like mud in any amount, just turn the page—you are still a good mother.

If you don't mind a little mud, and remember your own mud-pie days with pleasure, let your children have pie pans or coffee cans for mixing.

If it's a hot day, you can squirt them off with the hose before they come into the house. Dish pans or planter boxes (sans plants) are wonderful containers for mud.

Old swimming suits make
good mud costumes.

Leave a space in your yard for your children to dig. Provide garden hand tools such as a trowel, cultivator, and sprinkler.

Gravel

Gravel has a particular fascination for children. They love its coarse texture and, if it is a few inches deep, will sit and run their hands through it or scoop it into piles. A gravel path from the sandbox to the playhouse makes good use of this material.

Gravel doesn't stick to   Gravel rivers or lakes will
clothes and hands.   hold water longer than
                             sand ones do.

SOMETHING TO SPLASH IN

A rubber tire cut in half will make two rivers to float boats.

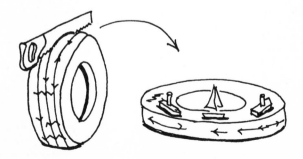

Some like their water coming up.

And some like it coming down.

SOMETHING TO SWING ON

Pump Swings

The pump swing is highly recommended for children under five years old for the following reasons.
1. A two-year-old can get on and off the swing by himself.
2. No one says "Push me." The motion depends upon "pull with your arms, push with your feet."
3. Since it is made of light-weight wood and held together with ropes, it is safer than the ordinary swing made of board seat and chains or ropes.

4. The pump swing is often more than just a swing.
   Sometimes it is a bucking bronco.
   It is easy to ride sidesaddle.

   Or be a trapeze performer.

The twister—one child sits on the swing while another child turns
            him in circles until, the three ropes are twisted
            several times. The child stands back while the child
            in the swing unwinds.

Two-man act—one child sits on the seat and the other child stands
            on the foot bar, facing the seated child.

Rubber Tires

A rubber tire hung in the usual fashion

A flying saucer effect.

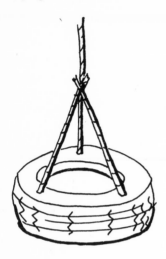

Other Swings

Canvas seat swings are safe, durable, and especially designed for those who like to swing on their stomachs.

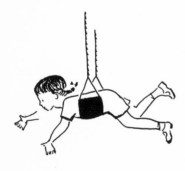

A gunny sack stuffed partially with sawdust, sand, and straw goes very well with big old oak trees.

Some can swing from a knotted rope, one knot every 12"-18".

SOMETHING TO PUSH

It is easier for children under five to have things to push, rather than pull, such as a wagon. These are all good "push" toys:

Wheelbarrows
Baby buggies—one that the child has outgrown is better than the toy-store selection for dolls
Strollers—same as above
Inner tubes
Grocery carts—secondhand from the grocery store
Dollies—secondhand or new

A Punching Bag

A burlap bag or canvas bag filled with sawdust is for pushing and punching. Tie a rope around the top of the bag and hang from tree.

When sawdust gets wet it is like a rock, so don't leave it out in the rain.

A pillow case can be used if other bags are not accessible.

9

An old cushion or bed
pillow is a ready-made
punching bag.

SOMETHING TO JUMP ON

Dig a hole or fill one that's already there with sawdust or tan-bark. (Tanbark is shavings from oak which is used in the process of leather tanning. Its advantages are that it is a quick ground cover, it is soft, and it doesn't track on your feet.)

Jump in it   or over it.

An old spring and mattress makes a wonderful jumping bed. If you keep it out of the rain. If you don't mind it's being unsightly.

Old car seats   and   Airplane inner tubes.

SOMETHING TO CLIMB

A Homemade Jungle Gym (giant sawhorse)

If you can make one between six and eight feet long and four to five feet high, so much the better. It must be at least four feet high in order to make it worth the crosspieces that make the ladder that provide the climb.

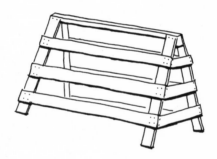

A jungle gym next to a fence is
a good place to see what's going
on next door.

Leave one end open, cover with a big blanket, and it becomes a tent.

It is big enough for chairs and tables. Add a few pots and pans and children will set up housekeeping.

A train.

A zoo.

Indians surrounding the white men.

Walking Board

A 1" x 12" board is flexible and springy and good for jumping on.

A 2" x 12" board is sturdier, but stiffer and heavy to move around.

The length of the board can be from 6 to 12 feet.

Crosspieces nailed on one side of the board at intervals give a ladder effect and make it stronger.

Children adjust the walking board to any level of the jungle gym they feel up to.

The walking board and the jungle gym make a good bridge for the troll to hide under when children play "Three Billy Goats Gruff."

Seesaw Board

A board 4' long, 8" wide, and 1" thick, with cleats on one side, is chiefly for the teeter-totter board used with small sawhorses (see below). However, your child will find many uses for this board.

Small Sawhorses

See-Saw Margery Daw with a small sawhorse (12" high) and the seesaw board.

Two sawhorses (12" high) and the seesaw board for a low bridge.

Two sawhorses (20" high) and a suitable length of wood, such as a door, make an excellent table.

Ladders

If you don't want to build a ladder, one from an old bunk bed is ideal for small children.

A jungle gym under a tree is a good ladder for climbing into the tree.

Tree House

Mostly fathers build tree houses. And fathers who build tree houses don't need instructions. Good additions to a tree house are: a pulley, a suitcase, or a basket that lowers on a rope.

It's a good idea to plant a tree.
It grows even while you are sleeping.

SOMETHING TO LIE ON

Any frame with spring and mattress. With casters, it is even better.

A chaise longue
A cot
A hammock
Just a mattress

OTHER THINGS TO PUT IN YOUR BACK YARD COULD BE:

An old car with wheels and doors off
An old rowboat (excellent sandbox)
A surplus navy life raft (for sand, water, or mud)
A tent

GOOD COMBINATIONS OF PLAY EQUIPMENT

A giant sawhorse with one end open, walking boards, smaller sawhorses, and a wooden ladder. A large packing box.

Swing set: One pump swing, one canvas swing, a wooden ladder on the end, a knotted rope of large diameter. A supporting structure is necessary, of course.

PLAYHOUSES AND PLAYHOUSE EQUIPMENT

A draped card table (or any table the child can get under).

These children got two sheets to call their own, and cut windows and doors.

A packing box—the bigger the better. Cut windows and doors.

It can be simple or fancy.

The corner of a 6' fence is two sides of a playhouse.

Fathers can build playhouses. And children can help them build, which is half the fun.

A playhouse is a good place to keep toys and bikes out of the rain. Children, too.

Design the playhouse after your own home. Or one you wish you had.

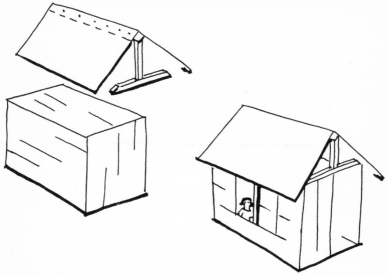

Mothers can make this playhouse: Sew two sheets together, hang over a clothesline and weight with bricks.

Or this one: Drape a wooden clothes dryer with a sheet.

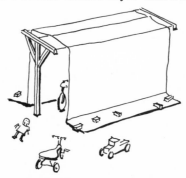

Large packing crates (which are partly made of cardboard) are good temporary playhouses.

Playhouse equipment from your kitchen: Egg beater, strainer, measuring cups and spoons, spatulas, pancake turner, pie pans, muffin tins, coffee cans, cocoa cans, frozen orange-juice cans, bouillon tins, sifters, a dustpan and brush, empty egg cartons, and empty cereal boxes.

Real sinks and stoves (secondhand) are inexpensive, and help make a playhouse a home. But orange-crate equipment is good, too.

Orange-crate Stove—Coffee-can lids painted black for burners. Spools for knobs. Oven doors are top and bottom knocked out of another crate, either hinged or secured with strips of inner tubing.

Cupboard—Imported wine or Scotch boxes sometimes have wooden dividers. Hang with two screen hooks and eyes.

Orange-crate Sink

Place an enameled pan between two orange crates. Nail the side of the crates to the playhouse or fence, but leave the pan free for dumping.

BOXES

Transportation with Boxes

Airplane: Insert wings through slots cut in box. A smaller box is the body and tailpiece. Cut smaller slots in this box.

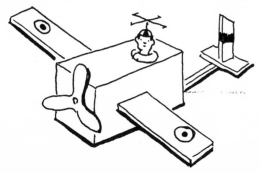

Boat: Fortunately for you, a preschool child's imagination allows him to believe that a boat does not need to rock. A wooden box with one or two seats in it is a good boat. Hang wooden ping-pong paddles on the side.

Car: An old steering wheel is attached to the box. Two coffee-can lids are on the front for headlights. Cars need casters.

Filling station: Attach three or four feet of garden hose to a heavy box which has been set into the ground, or on a wooden platform.

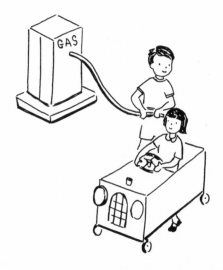

Train: The engine should be larger than the rest of the cars. Put a two-pound coffee can on top for the smokestack, and two one-pound cans on the front for headlights. A cowcatcher could be built on the front, and a bell attached for the engineer to ring. The coal car is an empty car. The cattle car is a slatted box.

If the cars are on casters they can be pulled easily. They make wonderful storage boxes for blocks and small toys.

USES FOR WOODEN WINE OR SCOTCH BOXES

(Available at liquor stores where imported liquor is sold—and they're usually free. Their advantage is sturdiness and durability. If they start to look shabby, give them another coat of paint.)

Circus wagon: Insert dowels through holes which have been bored all the way through the top, and only part way through the bottom. Bore two more holes in the top of the box for a handle made from clothesline rope.

Circus wagons carry very tame domestic animals for a short time and very tame stuffed animals for a long time.

Cupboard: If you get the kind of wine or Scotch box which has the wooden dividers that slide out, then you have a ready-made cupboard.

Stool: Just right for seating three-year-olds at low tables.

If it weren't for many colors of paint, this equipment wouldn't add to your back yard.

19

BARRELS

A stand is necessary.

> With both ends taken out, they are fun to crawl through.
> A good hide-out when only one end is open.
> Add a saddle, have a horse (most children will ride bareback).
> A good entrance into a playhouse.

NAIL KEGS

Indian drum

To keep toys and
blocks in.

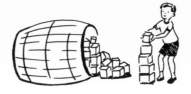

A chair

Base for table

ORANGE CRATES
(plus nail and hammer and saw)

Love seat

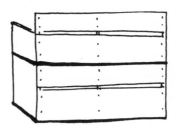

Sink and cupboard

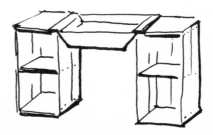

Store or carnival

Library

Dressing table

Dollhouse

Room dividers

Half-inch molding helps make
orange crates look less like
orange crates.

A TABLE

A smooth door put on a frame so it is reversible is a good plan.

One side could be painted with blackboard paint. The other could be covered with oilcloth or linoleum, or painted with a bright enamel.

If enamel is used, design the table with landing fields for airplanes, and rivers or lakes for boats.

The alphabet or numbers could border the table.

A piece of plywood over two small sawhorses also makes a good table.

RAIN, RAIN, GO AWAY!

But if it just goes on raining . . .

This chapter is about activities the child especially likes whether he is two years old or four years old. The activities which employ items everyone has around the house come first in this section.

In many of the activities, the mother needs to help the child get started (such as measuring the flour, salt, and water for the dough).

In others, she needs to show the child how the results are accomplished (as in spatter painting or paint blobs).

In others (such as clay), the mother can add the finishing touches by having the piece glazed and fired.

It's enough to do these things, whether or not you end up with a finished product. The fun is in the doing, as you will see.

THINGS TO DO

These suggestions require few materials, little clean-up, and once you have given the child the general idea for the use of the material, he can carry on from there.

Plain or Colored Toothpicks

Toothpicks are fun to arrange on a table in different designs. Sticking toothpicks into a dry sponge or scouring pad provides entertainment for very little children. Children can poke toothpicks into a potato, onion, cucumber, lemon or apple, to make an animal, a person, or a porcupine.

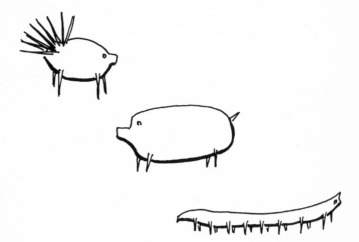

Bean or Cracker Pictures

Children can make designs on a table top with dry beans (such as navy or lima), or oyster or triangle crackers, or any combination of these.

Pipe Cleaners

Pipe cleaners have become popular recently, and come in assorted colors. Some preschoolers can made pipe-cleaner figures and dolls. Pipe cleaners can also be fashioned into handcuffs, eyeglasses, necklaces and rings, chains, handles for Easter or May-Day baskets, and Christmas-tree decorations (see Holidays section).

Colored Chalk

Colored chalk is fun on blackboards or pretty on paper. But it is especially effective on paper towels or paper plates which have been dampened.

Another Way: The next time the colored chalk is out, try dipping it in a glass of water before applying to the paper.

Pencils and Crayons

A four-year-old will discover that if he holds two crayons in his hand, he can make two marks on his paper with one movement.

Fringing Burlap

Burlap is so loosely woven that children can unravel it easily. Start with a small square (say 6" x 6") and let the child fringe the sides. If he likes to do this, he could make gifts of coasters and place mats (see "Christmas" in the Holidays section).

Felt on Felt

Glue a piece of felt on one side of a square of plywood or heavy cardboard (it should be at least 12" x 12"). Cut smaller pieces of felt into circles, squares, triangles, rectangles, or any shape you want. Shifting the arrangements into many patterns is obviously the fun here.

If you buy enough felt for the board, you can get the smaller pieces from old hats.

Sewing

Four-year-olds can sew large buttons onto a piece of cloth or cardboard. If you draw a chalk line where they are supposed to sew, small children can follow this line surprisingly well.

Soap Bubbles

Put liquid detergent in a paper or plastic cup and dilute with water. Use soda straws to blow bubbles. An outdoor activity unless you confine it to the kitchen or bathtub.

Cornmeal Sandbox

Partially fill a suit box with cornmeal and provide sieves, measuring cups, spoons, but no water (unless you want cornmeal pies!). The child can work while standing at a card table. Put a large shower curtain under the table.

Cornmeal is something like soft sand.

Collage

This is a technique of art which is especially suitable for children because it has so many possibilities. A child's interest is bound to hold when he is set before a collection of paper, metallic papers, paste, feathers, ribbons, soda straws, scotch tape, excelsior, colored sequins, and scraps of material. And he is sure to turn out an original picture. The idea is to have the collection of treasures on one side, a bottle of mucilage on the other, and a sheet of paper in the middle.

Start a box for collages. Use the materials listed above, and also watch for other suitable materials to add to the box such as: toothpicks, pipe cleaners, hairpins, string, rubber bands, colored stars, and cotton.

Children will add to the collection by contributing leaves, grasses, pine needles, shells, colored paper, candy and gum wrappers, and lollipop sticks.

When a child finds that certain objects do not stick well with glue or paste, suggest that scotch tape or gummed paper be used to hold the object in place. This is the only type of supervision necessary.

For an effective "canvas" for the collage, many kinds of materials may be used, such as colored construction paper (from stationery and variety stores), brown wrapping paper, cardboard, or a number of textiles, such as a piece of sheet or burlap thumbtacked to a base.

String Pictures

Have a bowl of thin paste solution (flour and water) for the child to dip pieces of colored string or yarn and press on colored paper.

Paste Recipes

School paste is a little expensive, especially when small children often finger paint with it, and many like its flavor. Here are some ways to make paste.

1. ½ cup flour and water mixed together until smooth and the consistency of heavy cream.
2. Wheat-paste flour (wallpaper paste) added to water which has been put into the bowl first. This is the same recipe as for finger painting (see below).
3. To make 1 pint of paste that will last indefinitely, dissolve ½ ounce of alum (which may be obtained from a drugstore) in 1 pint of warm water. Let stand until cold. Add flour slowly until it is as thick as heavy cream. Add ½ teaspoon powdered resin (also from the drugstore), and a few whole cloves to give it a spicy clean smell and make it taste better. Bring this mixture to a boil, stirring constantly, until it is thick.

Always use a clean spoon to dip the paste out of the jar.
Bacteria cause mold to form.

The child may make something which you or he want to keep. But certain activities are entertaining whether or not he ends up with a result.

Potter's Clay

Mostly, clay is to be pounded and punched, without the aid of tools. Possible exceptions might be a 10c rolling pin, and a popsicle stick for cutting. It is best to play with clay on nonporous materials such as linoleum, oil cloth, tile, or Formica-top breakfast tables.

Clay is a good investment. It is only 10c a pound (from a potter) and 35c a pound from stationery stores. Should it become hard, a small amount of water added and allowed to absorb will make it as good as new.

Children can make their own cereal bowl by pressing clay over an inverted wooden salad bowl. When the clay is dry, it will shrink from the bowl. It is ready to be fired, glazed, and fired again.

If you make something for your child
out of clay, he will no longer be
satisfied with what he can do, and
he will want you to continue to create
things for him.

But mostly clay is to be pounded and punched, rolled into balls, or rolled out like snakes and thrown back into the stone crock. If you don't have a stone crock, a plastic bag inside a potato-chip can with the lid on tight will do.

Dough

Most children prefer dough to clay "because you can make it pretty colors and it's not so sticky." Dough is 3 cups of flour, 2 cups of salt, and 1 cup of water. This recipe serves four children generously and six adequately. If the dough is sticky, add flour on the table where the child is playing and let him work it in.

You may want to color the whole batch one color, or divide it and have several colors. (Use food coloring or powdered poster paint.) A child can discover that his blue wad and his red wad, when mixed together, make a purple wad. He found this out with water paints and finger paints, but didn't know it would be true here, too.

Dough has advantages over clay in that it is spongy and resilient and will not stick to the oil cloth.

Rollers are important here.

Raisins can be added and the dough can be "baked" inside muffin tins or small pie pans in a play oven.

When dough is wrapped in a plastic bag, it will keep for several weeks without refrigeration. A tablespoon of salad oil will keep it soft and pliable. Add flour if necessary.

If the child has made something he wants to keep, it will take several days to dry, but it becomes almost as hard as plaster of Paris.

Wallpaper Cleaner

This material is pink and can be bought in small cans from the hardware store. It is very pliable, doesn't stick to hands, and children discover that it makes very funny false noses, which will stay on for a few minutes. After being exposed to the air for a time, it will become somewhat crumbly.

Modeling Clay

Modeling clay comes in many colors, never hardens, and needs no special care. It can be found in variety, dime, and stationery stores. It is too hard to be recommended as a suitable material for children under five, but no household should be without some. Uses for modeling clay are mentioned throughout this book.

Paints and Painting Smocks

Smocks are to wear while you are doing messy work.

Father's shirts go over heavy winter clothes.

Mother's blouses fit three - year - olds.

A shirt or blouse is a smock only after it has been put on backwards and buttoned down the back.

This is a picture of an oilcloth smock lying on the ground.

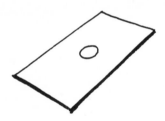

Here is the smock on an easel painter.

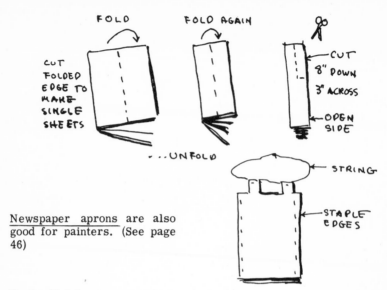

Newspaper aprons are also good for painters. (See page 46)

Poster Paint

An investment of four cans of powdered poster paint in red, yellow, blue and white will make many more colors when mixed together. When several colors get mixed, the tone will be inescapably brown. Brown is a very nice color, but if the child is using more than one color, suggest that he use a different brush for each can of paint. The brush should have a wide handle and stout bristles (No. 12 water color at stationery stores is good). Frozen orange-juice cans make excellent paint cans. One heaping teaspoon of the powdered paint and about 4 tablespoons of water make a fairly thick paint, not so likely to run, and the color will be bright. Food coloring can also be used for making color. (Powdered poster paint can be bought in stationery stores for about 90c a can.)

White is important because pink is a favorite color. Red and white make pink.

Blue and yellow make green. Blue and red make purple. Yellow and red make orange.

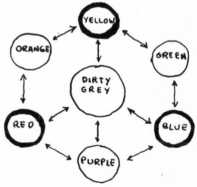

The smaller the child, the bigger the brush.

Children can paint old newspapers, wrapping paper, newsprint, butcher paper, or cloth. Newsprint is the best material. Newsprint is newspaper not yet printed. It comes in sheets or rolls and can be obtained from your newspaper office. It can be purchased in stationery stores for 25c a pound and it comes in various sizes.

Portfolios

For the child who makes many pictures, a place to keep all his work is important. A very simple envelope-type portfolio can be made by folding three sheets of newsprint and stapling along the two sides, leaving the top open. Write the child's name on the front and let him add a few touches of his own.

Paste or staple two of the child's paintings on two pieces of poster board. "Hinge" the boards with yarn, tied in three places. (Buy poster board at stationery stores.)

Easel

Even a mother can make an easel. Hinge together two pieces of plywood, approximately 20" x 24". (Get plywood from a lumber yard.) Attach trays to hold paint cans. Paper can be held in place with spring-type clothes pins.

Cover the plywood with several coats of shellac for easy cleaning.   or —   You might paint one side of the easel with blackboard paint.

When the easel is standing, it should not be more than a head taller than the child.

Looking at an easel.

Sideways.

Some children find painting at easels annoying because the paint runs down the paper. Show how to wipe excess paint off the brush onto the side of the can before applying to paper.

Paint on the floor or on the table if you do not have an easel.

Sponge Painting

Cut a cellulose sponge into one- or two-inch squares. Put the dry sponges in a pan of water. Explain to the child that he should squeeze out most of the water from the sponge before he dips it into the powdered poster paint. A muffin tin with different colors in each mold makes a good container for the paint. Suggest to the child that he pat, rather than rub, the squares onto the paper. The part-dry, part-wet paint leaves an interesting texture, not obtained by any other method of painting. A separate piece of sponge should be used for each color. Sponge paintings look very attractive on walls and can be used to wrap gifts, to cover cans for plants, and to wrap around gallon ice-cream cartons which make durable wastepaper baskets.

Stick Painting

Dip ends of short pieces of dowels, blocks, or triangular shaped pieces of wood into paint, which has been mixed in a bowl, and press on paper.

Paint Blobs

Use a spoon and place a very small blob of poster paint, which has been mixed in a bowl, in the center of a piece of paper toweling. (Any paper will do, but this is very handy.) Fold the paper in half and smooth with fingers. Then fold the paper again and smooth. Open the paper to see the results! After the child gets the idea he will experiment with two or three blobs of paint, perhaps different colors, and the results are very colorful. This is fun and easy; the comments made by the children when they see the results are very interesting.

Potato Stamping

Cut a small potato in half and with a paring knife carve a design in the surface of one of the halves. Cut away the area of the potato you don't want to print. The child can dip the potato in a shallow dish of colored paint, and apply (like a rubber stamp) to any type of paper or fabric. Use the paper for tapestry or gift wrapping; children can stamp these designs on small cards that can be used as Christmas cards.

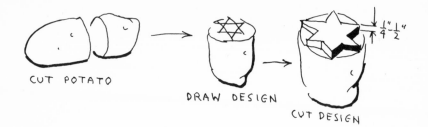

CUT POTATO

DRAW DESIGN

CUT DESIGN

$\frac{1}{4}" - \frac{1}{2}"$

Spatter Painting

Help the child begin this process. He dips a toothbrush into a bowl of colored paint, and holds the toothbrush in his left hand. Tell him to pull the bristles <u>toward</u> him with the spoon or popsicle stick which he holds in his right hand, so the paint will spatter upon the paper. Use a different toothbrush for each color of paint. More than one color makes more interesting spatters.

To make a silhouette, lightly paste a leaf, or figure cut from a magazine, on the paper and then spatter.

Try spatter painting an old sheet. If it is to be used later in the doll's bed or for a kerchief, a Rit dye would make it permanent.

Instead of a toothbrush, a sprinkler bottle or spray gun may be used.

Another Method: Dip the toothbrush into the bowl of paint and rub across a small piece of door screen. Hold the screen about four or five inches from the paper.

Painting on Material

Old sheets or dishtowels are good for this. Use thumbtacks to hold the material in place and paint with brush, sponges, or potato stamps (see above). If the child is painting on a table, use several thicknesses of newspaper under the material.

Painting Balloons

Blow up a balloon, tie it with a string, and let the child paint it. If mother takes brush in hand, it could bear a message and become an invitation (see Children's Birthdays and Parties in chapter VERY SPECIAL EVENTS). Note: the paint peels off if the balloon is deflated.

Painting Over Crayon

After the child has colored a picture with crayons, have him paint over the entire picture with poster paint. As the paint does not cover the wax crayon markings, interesting effects may be achieved.

Painting on a Blotter

This is fun because of the fascination of watching how rapidly the blotter absorbs the paint.

Painting With Water

Small children enjoy painting porch furniture, the house, or fences with a bucket of water and a three-inch paint brush. And it is particularly satisfying to paint thirsty, dry wood on a hot day.

Finger Painting

You probably haven't had finger paint for your children since you tried the old-fashioned recipe and spent the afternoon cooking up cornstarch, alum, glycerin, and water, and had to have canned salmon for dinner. But if you are ready to try again, the simple recipe is:

Put one cup of water into a bowl first. Add wheat-paste flour slowly and stir constantly until it is the consistency of whipped cream. Now you are ready to add coloring. Either add poster paint to the whole batch, or color each glob separately as you spoon it out on the butcher paper which has been dampened with a sponge.

Any glazed paper, such as shelf paper, will do.

Your butcher will sell you butcher paper for 15c a pound, and this is the best kind for finger painting. If you ask ahead, he will save you an inch or two on the roller, making it easier to handle. Stationery stores also sell butcher paper.

The hardware store sells wheat-paste flour (wallpaper paste). A five-pound supply will carry you through many finger paintings, and it will cost you about one dollar.

It is a good idea to roll the sleeves up on the smock as children paint with their fingers, hands, arms and elbows. Spreading the paper the full length and width of the table, instead of cutting it into squares, gives the child more freedom, and makes the clean-up job easier for you.

Have a pan or bucket of sudsy water
ready for hand washing when the child
is through with his finger painting.

Blocks and Carpentry

Wood has a particular fascination for children because of its many possibilities. Most children like to paint their boats, others like to sand them, others are not satisfied until there is no more space in which to pound another nail, and still others like to scrub their wood with soapy water and a vegetable brush. In their workshops children like to have a low table with a vise, hammer, saw, soft wood and lots of nails. It could eventually include a screwdriver, pair of pliers, ruler, pencil, sandpaper, and a brace and bit.

A good way to store tools: Paint the shape of each tool on a piece of plywood and hold with nails. Hang the plywood behind the workbench.

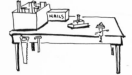

Or

Hang the tools from nails across the front of the work bench. This is better for small children as the tools are all within easy reach.

Children often need help in starting the nail into the wood. The same is true with the saw. (Toy saws will not cut wood properly. A real saw, such as a kitchen saw or a keyhole saw, is suggested.)

Children can make boats or airplanes or signs without much help. Or they can make sandpaper blocks for sanding, or for scraping together (see the section You Can Make Your Own Music).

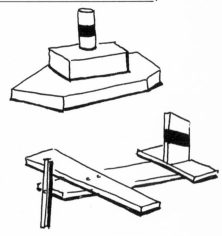

Roofing nails have a large head and are easy to hit. But you can't go wrong with fourpenny box nails.

Beginners can hammer tacks in a cake of soap.

Beginners can saw
cardboard boxes.

Wood and blocks: Lumber for children's workshops is available at
lumber companies where there are always odds
and ends under the power saw; or ask the supervisor of any construction job if you can scavenger
their scrap pile. Specially good pieces of wood
should be sanded and painted and used for blocks.
Another way to make blocks is by cutting a 2 x 4
into different lengths.

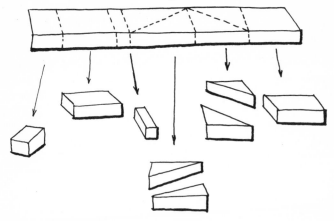

Hollow blocks: These blocks are recommended for small children
because of their light weight, long life, and the
variety of uses they offer. They are made by nailing
and gluing together two ends, a half an inch thick and
four sides of one-fourth inch plywood.

Cut an opening in two opposite sides for fingers.

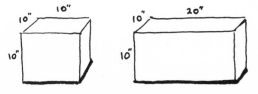

MAKING THINGS

Although the fun is in the doing, in these
activities you have a finished product, too.

In some of these suggestions, help from the mother or father is
essential. In most of them, it is on a partnership basis. For example,
the child decorates the flag and the mother attaches it to the pole.

What part you do and what part the child does depend on so many
things that the instructions do not indicate who does what.

Fishing Poles

Tie a piece of string to a length of doweling or a stick from a
tree. On the end of the string tie a magnet. The child can "catch"
bobby pins, nails, or other pieces of hardware on his pole.

Dumbells

Bore holes in two wooden croquet balls or good-sized solid
blocks. Connect with a six- or eight-inch piece of doweling.

Flags

Decorate pieces of old sheet or dishtowel and nail to a stick or
length of molding.

Golf Clubs

See "Ball Games" in chapter VERY SPECIAL EVENTS under
Games.

Indians

Indian war paint: Lipstick is the favorite (use cold cream to protect
the skin and make removal easy). Colored chalk,
poster paint, food coloring and washable inks also
make good war paint.

Indian Brave: Scotch tape one real feather or a pretend feather cut
from cardboard to the middle of the child's forehead.

Indian headdress: Rip a piece of sheet long enough to tie around the
child's head and wide enough to double. Cut
feathers from cereal boxes or stiff paper, and
staple or sew to the sheet.

Indian bows and arrows: Tie a string to each end of a green branch from a tree (no taller than the child). Tie the string taut enough so the branch will bend properly. Any small green twig with a slot cut in one end can serve as an arrow.

Quiver: See "Wax-paper tubes" in the section Things to Save and Why.

Wire Sculpture

Any type of wire that children can bend easily in their hands without the use of tools is best. After the child has played with his wire suspend it in his room. Figures to hang on the basic structure can be made of paper, pipe cleaners, twist 'ems, soda straws, or milk-bottle caps. If the basic structure is fairly simple and sturdy, the sculpture can change according to the season. Eggshells at Easter (how to blow eggs from the shell is described in the Holidays section under "Easter"), hearts for Valentines, and Christmas decorations are several suggestions.

Wire Jewelry

Children can twist and bend a piece of fine copper wire into many interesting shapes. Use as a brooch by fastening a small safety pin on the underneath side of their shirts or dresses. (Get copper wire from hardware store.)

Other Jewelry

String macaroni for necklaces and bracelets. (Macaroni can be colored by dipping in a bowl of food coloring for a moment and drying on a paper towel).

Crowns, necklaces or bracelets can be made by tying together dandelions, clover, or daisies.

Run a piece of elastic or ribbon through a button to tie on the finger for a ring.

For brooches use bottle tops with the cork on the under side of the shirt and the top on the outside. If the cork doesn't pry out easily, soak it for a few minutes in warm water.

THINGS TO MAKE WITH PAPER

Paper Tearing

Instead of using scissors, which are hard for small fingers to use anyway, try paper tearing, which is slowly twisting and turning a piece of paper as you tear it so that it will have an interesting design when completed.

Carbon Paper

Staple, or fasten with paper clips, two sheets of paper together with the carbon in between. Use a lead pencil to make pictures. For children who do not know the magic of carbon, this is a new experience.

Paper Chains

Cut colored construction paper into strips approximately one inch by five inches. Form a circle by pasting or stapling the ends together. Run the next strip through the first circle, staple ends together, and continue. It is hard for small children to get the idea of overlapping the ends.

Not this . . .

but this.

Paper Lantern

Fold a rectangular sheet of paper in half crosswise (8½" x 11"). Starting on the fold, cut one-inch strips to within one inch of the top.

It will help the child if you will draw a line at this inch mark to indicate where he should stop cutting. Either paste or staple the two lengthwise edges together. Fasten a strip over the top for a handle.

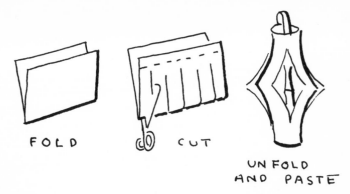

FOLD   CUT

UN FOLD
AND PASTE

Paper Fan

Pleat a rectangular sheet of paper by folding back and forth. Wind a rubber band several times around one end of folded pleats for a handle. Ease the pleats out a little, and fan!

Paper Hat

Fold a rectangular sheet of paper in half crosswise. From the folded end, fold the two corners to the center of the paper and within an inch or two from the bottom of the paper. Fold the open ends up, one on each side of the hat. Makes excellent use of an easel painting done on newsprint. Or use newspaper.

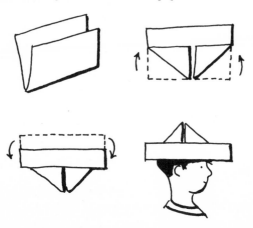

Paper Boat

— MAKE A "HAT" FROM 8" X 11" PAPER
THEN:

PEAK

END
PULL ENDS
TOGETHER

FOLD HERE SO
ENDS TOUCH
PEAK

PULL ENDS
TOGETHER

PULL APART

KEEP PULLING ...

UNTIL A BOAT APPEARS

Paper Airplane

Fold a piece of paper 8½" x 11" in half. Open the paper and fold down two corners at one end to meet the crease line, then fold again to the crease line. Then fold so that the two sides meet. Fold each side halfway back again.

Paper Snowflakes

Fold a square of paper in half, then in half again. Cut slashes, notches, or scallops, and unfold. (See "Christmas Decorations" in the Holidays section.)

Paper Spirals

Start with a circle of paper. It could be aluminum foil, metallic paper, or colored construction paper. From the outside draw a line around and around until it comes to the center. The child can follow this line with scissors. Fun to do any time, but they are especially for Christmas tree ornaments (see "Christmas Decorations" under Holidays).

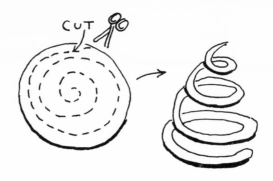

Jigsaw Puzzles

After the child has colored or painted his picture on a piece of cardboard (such as a shirt cardboard), cut it into four or five pieces and let him fit the picture together again. (See Stay-In-Bed Days.)

Paper Plates

Paper-plate clock: Mark numbers around the edge of the plate. Cut hands (one slightly longer than the other) and fasten in the center with a paper fastener. As you can see, the child can do little or nothing in making this project, but he will enjoy having the clock.

Paper-plate hat: Tie a ribbon on opposite sides of a paper plate. Tie the ribbons under the chin. Mostly for girls.

Paper-plate tambourine: This is described in the section You Can Make Your Own Music.

Paper-plate picture: Let the child color with crayon, colored chalk, or poster paint on both sides of a paper plate. Punch holes in the top of the picture, tie yarn through the holes, and hang it in his room. It is reversible.

Paper-bag Masks

Cut off a few inches or roll the bottom of a paper bag up so the top of the bag rests on the child's head. Measure where the eyes are and cut circles (take the bag off of his head first). Lengths of yarn can be glued on the top of the bag for hair, or soda straws cut in half and glued on to make whiskers. The child can color his mask as he likes. A spaceman can be made by cutting a large circle in the front of the bag and pasting a piece of cellophane over the opening (see "Halloween" in the Holidays section).

Shoe-box Train

Tie several shoe boxes together with short pieces of string. The child will pull the train with a long piece of string tied to the first box.

Parachute

Tie a string (12") around each corner of a paper napkin or man's handkerchief. Tie all four ends of string to a cork or small stick. Throw it into the air and it will sometimes come down slowly — parachute fashion.

Puppets

Sock puppet: Draw a face with chalk on a dark stocking or with a crayon on a white stocking and fit it over the child's hand.

Peanut puppet: After the peanuts have been eaten, put the shells on the ends of the fingers. You can make tiny faces with a pen point, but a face is not necessary.

Paper-bag puppet: Make a face or decorate a small paper bag as in Paper-bag Masks (above). Put over the child's hand, and secure with a rubber band around the wrist.

Newspaper Aprons

Stack six or seven double sheets of newpapers out flat on a table. Fold lengthwise in half, then in half again. To make the neck piece, cut a section 8" x 3" down across from the open side. Unfold and staple the paper together around all the sides except the bottom. Cut the bottom off several inches or to the calf of the child. Cut it in scallops, points, or fringe. Run a string through the top of the apron to go around the neck.

Paper Balloons

Blow up a big round balloon, and tie with string. Tear strips of newspaper about 1" x 6". Put a strip on the balloon, cover with flour-and-water paste, add the next strip so that it overlaps, paste, and continue until the balloon is completely covered. Hang the balloon by the string in a place where it will dry quickly. When it is thoroughly dry (this may take several hours) cover again with newspaper strips, this time using the comic section or sporting-green section of your newspaper (to make certain the balloon is covered completely with two layers). When it is dry, let the air out of the balloon, and you have a hollow ball. It can be sprayed with the new pressurized spray enamels, and then decorated with poster paints. It is ready for many uses.

Halloween Mask.

Mobile.

Giant Easter Egg

or Christmas Dec-
oration.

This is a project children are wildly enthusiastic about at first, but tire of quickly. Luckily, mothers become fascinated.

THINGS TO SAVE, AND WHY

If you save a thing for seven years you will find a use for it.

—Anonymous

THINGS TO SAVE, AND WHY

At first glance this chapter will seem to suggest that things be saved so that Mother may make them into toys and games for her child. In nearly all cases, however, there is a way in which the child can actively participate. He can soak labels off cans, fill a rattle with rocks he has collected, and go through the catch-all drawer in the kitchen to sort the treasures. So both mother and child find many every-day things which become materials for original creations.

Although you, not the child, will add to many of these things to save, some of them are good toys as is.

Oatmeal Boxes

Pull toys: Make a pull toy for the littlest one by filling the carton with marbles, rocks, jingle bells, bottle caps or sea shells. Punch a hole through the center of the ends of the box. Run a string through the holes and pull the string so the short end ties on the longer end about four inches from the box. Tie a loop on the end of the string for the child's hand.

Knitting box: Cover the box and the lid separately with wallpaper, colored paper, or a finger painting. Punch a hole in the lid after it is decorated, and do not make the mistake of pasting the lid to the box. Punch a hole on opposite sides of the box and use a pipe cleaner for the handle. This could be a Christmas gift for Aunt Lois or anyone who knits.

Drum: Paste or glue the open end to the box. Paste long triangles of colored construction paper around the box or color with poster paints and add a few Indian designs to make it look real. The child holds it under his arm or between his knees and beats on the end with his hands. (see You Can Make Your Own Music.)

Toilet-paper Tubes

Rattle: Put a wad of paper in the end of a toilet-paper tube, then fill it with rocks, small stones, or dried beans, and stuff more paper in the other end. It should be covered with plastic leather or oil cloth and glued tightly. (See You Can Make Your Own Music.)

Blower: Toilet-paper tubes make good noises when you blow through them (referred to as "woo-woo's" in the section You Can Make Your Own Music).

Favor: Fill the roller with a piece of bubble gum, some gumdrops, a shiny penny, a balloon, and wrap in a piece of crepe paper that extends over the ends an inch and a half. Twist the ends and tie with ribbons. All the treasures are safely inside. (See Children's Birthdays and Parties.)

Wax-Paper Tubes

Quiver: Cover the tube with plastic leather. Extend the leather on one end only and fold it under so the bottom end of the tube is covered, and the arrows don't fall out. A piece of rawhide thong (from the shoe-repair store) is then run through the top of the tube and hung over a boy's shoulder. This will make an authentic-looking quiver.

Sturdy Egg Cartons

Treasure chest: Each hole can hold the week's surprises and secrets—a few old nails, some marbles, jacks, golf balls, and rocks.

Game: Toss marbles and see how many you can get into the holes. For older children, paint numbers on the sides and keep score.

Shirt Cardboards

These are fun to color or paint or cut a jigsaw puzzle as described in the section Making Things. They can also be used as mats when you are mounting smaller pictures.

Wallpaper

Out-of-style wallpaper books, or rolls of wallpaper, or glueless wallpaper are all handy for many uses. You can color it, cut it, or cut it up and paste it in scrap books. Paste wallpaper inside an orange-crate dollhouse. Every side a different pattern makes a gay house.

White Bakery Bags

You can make three paper "party" hats from one bakery bag. Cut the bottom of the bag about two inches wide and it makes a headband. Decorate it any way you wish, but one way would be to paste paper feathers for an Indian headdress. Cut the next width about four inches wide, cutting notches across one side like a king's or queen's crown. The third hat is made from the bottom of the paper bag, and it fits nicely over the child's head. Roll up the cut edge about an inch to make it look better and fit better. All three hats stay on children's heads, if you get the right size of bakery bag.

Brown-paper Bags

Masks: A paper bag large enough to fit over the child's head can be rolled up around the bottom or can be cut off. Cut eyes, nose, and mouth and decorate to suit the occasion (see "Halloween" in Holidays section).

Puppets: Draw a face on a small paper bag. Put over the child's hand and secure the bag with a rubber band around the child's wrist. (See Making Things.)

Mesh Bags

Block bags: Bags that come filled with oranges, apples, and potatoes later become good block bags. You could keep small balls or dirty laundry in them too.

Ping-pong net: Rip open both sides of a mesh bag leaving the bottom of the bag intact. Extend the net between two straight-back chairs and hold with pipe cleaners.

Punching bag: Let the child tear and wad pieces of newspaper into balls about the size of a grapefruit. Stuff the balls in the mesh bag until it is full. Draw the string and knot it. The child can sit on it, throw it, jump on it or sleep on it.

Plastic Bags

Doll's wardrobe: The plastic bags that hold fresh fruit and vegetables in the grocery store are good for little girls who like to keep their doll's dresses neat and clean.

Rain hats: Roll up the bottom of the bag to fit the child's head.

Cottage-Cheese Cartons and Berry Boxes

May baskets and
Easter baskets: Cover the box with strips of colored crepe paper and paste or staple to hold. Wrap a cardboard handle with crepe paper, and staple to the sides of the box. (See "Easter" in Holidays section.)

Gallon Ice-Cream Cartons

Wastebaskets: Cover the carton with the wallpaper which only needs a wet sponge to make it stick, old greeting cards, or pictures from calendars or magazines. If you paste on a child's finger painting and spray it with clear shellac this will be even more his creation.

Shoe Boxes

Train: String the boxes together for a floor train.

Cigar Boxes

Doll bed: Remove the top of the box and paint it or cover it with material or paper. Add four spools for legs.

Supply box: Ideal for crayons, scissors, small bottle of glue. Also a good box for treasures.

Orange Crates and Boxes

Outdoor play equipment: Uses for these boxes have been described in the section, Outdoor Play Equipment.

CANS

Coffee Cans

Drum: How to make a drum is described in the section You Can Make Your Own Music.

Windbell: Use the lid of the coffee can. Punch several holes around the sides of the lid and attach paper clips, nails, or any small piece of hardware that will "jingle" when in motion. Hang in the wind. Transfer to the peach tree when the peaches are getting ripe. Very effective in discouraging blue jays.

Christmas decoration: Unwind the metal strip that opens the coffee can. It will look like an icicle and add glitter to your tree.
Warning: It is sharp—but seldom fatal.

Cocoa Cans

Bank: Remove the paper label and cut a slit in the tin lid.

Cans of Graduated Sizes

Nests: Start with a tall grapefruit-juice can or a large-size solid-pack tomato can, and fit cans into it down to the smallest which is usually a baby-food can. Remove the labels and paint them each a different color. For a small child, the bright silver of the can itself is enough.

Bouillon-Cube and Band-Aid Cans

Water play: These small cans are loved by small children for play either in the bathroom sink or in their playhouse.

Washboard

Musical washboard: Strumming on the washboard with thimbles on the fingers is a favorite instrument. (See You Can Make Your Own Music.)

Washing: Children like to scrub dolls' clothes or washrags this old-fashioned way.

Milk-Bottle Tops

Money: You can mark the tops 1c, 5c, 10c, $1.00, $5.00; however, children will use them for money just as they are. Remember to have something around which the child wants to buy and you are willing to sell.

Christmas decorations: Spread paste on both sides of the cardboard disc and dip in Christmas "snow" or glitter. Punch a hole and tie a string to it and hang it on the Christmas tree. (See "Christmas" in the Holidays section.)

Old Clothes and Jewelry

For dress-up: The choicest items for the girls are furs, gold party shoes, bag to match, gloves, sequin blouses and fancy aprons. Lots of old costume jewelry. For the boys there are army hats, shirts, medals and duffel bags. Father's old felt or straw, loud ties, vests, and men's black patent-leather shoes. Spats are appreciated by some, hip boots by others. Boys also like ladies' hats, purses, and shoes.

Felt Hats

For beanies: Cut the brim off father's old hat and turn up the edges. Cut scallops or notches. Add decorations, such as safety pins or campaign buttons. Cut decorations into the crown of the hat.

For designing: Cut circles, squares, triangles and strips, and the child can arrange according to his desires. A larger piece of felt can be used for the background. (See the section Things To Do.)

Feathers

Indian Brave: Staple a feather or feathers on a strip of white sheet and tie around the child's forehead. Get feathers at the poultry store.

Collage: See Things To Do.

Buttons

Sewing: Sewing buttons on cloth or cardboard is fun for children. (See Things To Do.)

Whizzer: String one hole of button on a piece of string about a foot long. Twirl the string several times and then stretch.

Spools

Legs for doll bed: Glue four spools to the bottom of a cigar box for the doll's bed (see preceding).

Stove burner controls: Spools can be glued or nailed on the front of an orange-crate stove for pretend burner controls (see Outdoor Play Equipment).

For stringing: String spools on a long shoelace and tie around the neck.

Corks

Painting: Try painting with corks instead of a brush.

Stamping: The stamp is made by cutting away the area you don't want to print. Dip the cork in paint or ink or ink pad and apply to paper or fabric.

Dolls: Corks can be stuck in small bottles as heads for dolls. Make faces with pen and ink. Wrap a piece of material around the neck of the bottle and hold in place with pipe cleaners.

Pipe Cleaners

Uses for pipe cleaners are described in the section Things To Do.

Jar Lids

For picture frames: This round metal cap can hold a piece of art work or picture of the family, a friend, or the child himself.

As stirrups: For the play horse made from a barrel, use jar lids for stirrups.

Ring toss: The bedpost is a good target for this game. The rubber seals used on the old-style jars were better for this, but are a rarity these days.

Easel tray: Nail jar lids to the easel tray. They help keep paint cans steady.

Toothbrushes

Spatter painting: Dip old toothbrushes in paint and with a spoon or popsicle stick brush the bristles toward you—to spatter the paint away from you. (See "Spatter Painting" in the Things To Do section.)

Candle Stubs

Candles: Old candles can be melted down and poured into molds for more candles. Use a piece of string for the wick. Good molds are round ice-cream cartons and square milk-bottle cartons. Food coloring or melted crayons can determine the color. But do not set these candles on your good furniture without a dish.

Aluminum Foil

Christmas decorations: Heavier foil, such as the kind frozen chicken pies come in, can be cut into stars, spirals, or cornucopias. Household aluminum can be used for wrapping walnuts (to be hung from the tree with ribbons), wrapping packages, or coffee cans filled with cookies or a plant. (See "Christmas" in Holidays section.)

Ham Bones

Napkin rings: When the center ham-bone ring is clean and dry, it can be painted with bright enamel. (See "Christmas" in the Holidays section.)

Wishbones

Decorations: If wishbones from all fowl are saved throughout the year, painted with silver or gold enamel, hung from the tree or tied to Christmas or birthday gifts, you can wish on them with certain success.

Rubber Tiles

As roads: When rubber or asphalt squares are stretched out in a line on the floor, they make a wonderful road to run small cars and trucks on.

Playhouse equipment: When these squares are fitted inside an orange-crate sink or cupboard, they give the kitchen a "custom-made" look that is very easy to keep clean.

Broomsticks

Trapeze: A trapeze can be easily constructed by tying two pieces of rope on either end and hanging from something that is secured and sturdy.

Horses: A broomstick or mop stick is a horse or a witch's stick, just as it is. If your child likes his horse to have a head, one can be made easily from a man's sock stuffed with cotton batting or old nylons.

Rubber Hose

Fireman: A length of from five to ten feet supplies the equipment necessary to put out the fire.

Filling station: Secure a smaller piece, approximately three feet, to a sturdy box you have designed for the purpose of being a gasoline station. (See Outdoor Play Equipment.)

Alarm Clock

Children can have a wonderful time with clocks that are no longer dependable, but still have working parts.

Old Typewriter

Besides being educational, a typewriter is wonderful fun and an old one will keep children from using the untouchable one which is yours. But this is a rare item. You can try secretarial schools, your typewriter dealer, or a used furniture-curio shop.

Wheels, Tires, Inner Tubes, and Tire Pumps

Children will invent their own games around these choice objects.

COOKING

Warm water + bouillon cube = Soup

COOKING

A great part of the child's life is centered around FOOD. And so is mother's: even with freezers, frozen foods, instant puddings and box mixes, mothers are still spending a lot of time in the kitchen.

Since children enjoy anything that transforms in the making, they love to help in the preparation of food. Sometimes they can make something special for themselves, and sometimes they can help in preparing the family meal. The list has been divided into these two categories, and with few exceptions, these are all things children can make without using the stove.

How Children Can Fix Their Own Lunch or Snack

Colored water: Very young children delight in drinking water which has been colored with a few drops of food coloring. They are usually happy with this until they find out about Kool-Aid.

Colored ice: Freeze colored water in an ice-cube tray. When you add sticks (toothpicks, skewers, or sucker sticks), you have popsicles.

Jello: Jello can be dissolved with hot water from the tap instead of boiling water from the stove. Some children like to drink their jello before it hardens; some like it straight from the package.

Soup: A bouillon cube dissolved in a cup of hot tap water makes soup. They can stir to their heart's content.

Toast and sandwiches: They can spread their own peanut butter and jelly. They can butter toast from an automatic toaster, and with a little cinnamon and sugar have cinnamon toast. They can peel and chop hard-cooked eggs for an egg-salad sandwich.

Milk and cocoa: Children can add any prepared chocolate mixture to milk for hot or cold drinks.

Frozen juices: Once the can is open and the child can count to three, he can mix orange juice or lemonade.

Fruit salad: They can cut pineapple chunks, pieces of apple and bananas, peaches or pears with a silver knife.

Vegetable salad: Foods that are often not attractive to children, such as peas, green beans, asparagus and beets, take on a new look after the child has arranged them on skewers or toothpicks.

Popcorn: What the child can contribute here depends upon the type of popper you use. Popping corn is a family affair.

How Children Can Help With Dinner

Bread: The child can help in the kneading of bread and rolls. He will like a chunk to roll out and pound and bake in his own miniature pan.

Pie: In this case, children must have their own piece of dough to work with and have nothing to do with the crust you are serving for dessert.

Vegetables: Children can use vegetable scrapers very well in peeling carrots or potatoes. They like to shell peas especially well, and can snip the ends off beans with scissors.

Meatballs: It is great fun for the child to start with a bowl of ground meat and mix an egg, bread crumbs, salt and pepper and onion with both hands. They will find making porcupines (rolling the meatballs in uncooked rice) even more entertaining.

Food grinders: Most foods are too difficult for children to grind. But making bread crumbs out of dried bread is fun and easy.

Instant puddings: Two cups of milk added to the powdered mix can be stirred with a spoon or shaken in a plastic container with a tight lid.

Box mixes: Corn bread is particularly successful because it requires very little mixing.

Refrigerator cookies: A cheese cutter is a good aid in making uniform slices.

Cracking and shelling walnuts: Several thicknesses of newspaper on the floor and a tack or claw hammer is standard equipment. This is a kitchen job that is very popular with preschoolers. If you can't keep up with the supply, let them give Grandmother a jar of shelled nuts for Christmas.

Special goodies:
    a. Marshmallows, and gumdrops stuck into an apple with toothpicks, make dolls, animals, or just pretty designs.
    b. They can stuff prunes and dates with nuts and roll in powdered sugar.
    c. Decorate cookies with nuts, colored sugar, raisins or chocolate drops.
    d. Spread chocolate frosting on graham crackers.
    e. Cupcakes are more fun if they have surprises in the middle of them. Good surprises are a maraschino cherry or half a walnut.

YOU CAN MAKE YOUR OWN MUSIC

People who make no noise are dangerous.

—La Fontaine

YOU CAN MAKE YOUR OWN MUSIC

Some children at a very early age reveal a musical talent that parents often overlook.

Rhythms at the table are very popular with young children. Beating the table with the silverware, hitting full glasses of milk with their forks, and blowing bubbles in their tomato juice are but a few. Others are rocking on their elbows and kicking table legs with their feet—and you know a lot more.

Musical instruments around the house are really scarce. If there is a piano, it's not to be banged on. Father's violin is on the top shelf and even <u>he</u> doesn't get it out any more because the children are not content to let just <u>him</u> play it.

You may want to channel this talent in a more civilized fashion. The instruments described below are fun to make and fun to use for accompanying dancing or records. They are also good in parades. Chances are you have the entire rhythm band in your own house, though you may have to go to Grandma's cellar for the washboard.

Tambourine

1. Staple two paper plates together facing each other. Tie four or five jingle bells or any pieces of hardware that will jangle when the tambourine is in motion. Let the children color the paper plates with crayons. They will have a surprisingly long life, since paper plates tend to pop back into shape, even after being stepped on.

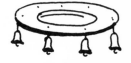

2. Tie "jinglers" to the hollow ring of an old embroidery hoop.

Rattles

1. Fill a baby-food can with seeds, beans, rice, gravel or whatever is handy. Cover the open end with any scrap of material. A piece of plastic, oilcloth or leatherette serves well for this purpose. Secure it by wrapping a rubber band around the end several times. Be sure to let the children help you make this rattle so they will know what's inside before you get the rubber band on.

2. A toilet-paper roller can be filled in the same way with the same things and stuffed with paper at either end and then wrapped so that the extended ends of material can be twisted and tied.

3. Pierce a hole in a dry gourd and fill with beans, rice, shot, or rocks. Tape the hole with adhesive.

4. A clam shell (if you can find a clam shell) filled and glued together, makes a good rattle.

5. Partially fill a small bottle with pebbles and cork it.

Triangle

A horseshoe hung by a cord and struck with a long nail is very effective, since it produces a clear ringing sound.

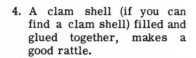

Cymbals

While two pot covers struck together sound like nothing so much as two pot covers struck together, the child thinks they make wonderful cymbals. Tying ribbon or yarn around the handles for decoration will help keep the two you have donated for the occasion separate from your own good lids.

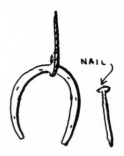

Guitars

Stretch rubber bands around a shoe box or cigar box and pluck or strum.

Harps

Stretch rubber bands around the back of a straight chair and pluck or strum.

Musical Comb

Wrap a piece of tissue paper over a comb and hum.

Rhythm Sticks

If you don't have ten-inch lengths of doweling around, you'll find you have something similar in handles from broken "pushers," long-gone toy lawnmowers, or chair rungs. When someone in your family has cymbals and someone else has the triangle, it's sometimes kind of hard to get anyone to think that rhythm sticks are very interesting. If you tie strips of crepe paper at the end for a "wand" effect and a swishy noise, these will seem more desirable.

Chimes

Three flower pots that fit inside each other and can "nest" when not in use make chimes. String them together on a rope—clothesline rope works best—and tie a big knot so it will not slip through the hole. Strike the chimes with a nail or piece of metal. It makes kind of a dull thud, and though they look attractive, it's hard to make much music out of clay.

Sandpaper Blocks

Thumbtack sandpaper on blocks of wood. Swish together.

Bass Music

Blow into an empty pop bottle.

Musical Washboard

Find as many thimbles as you can and let the child put them on his fingers and rub them across the bumps of the washboard. Popsicle sticks and wooden ice-cream spoons make good "strummers" too.

Drums

1. Cut strips of colored paper in triangle shapes and paste on an oatmeal box. Either hold the box between the knees and tap on one end with the fingers, or run a string through a hole near the edge at each end and hang it around the neck.

2. A two-pound coffee can may be opened at both ends and inner tubing "rounds" cut to overlap an inch or two. With a punch make holes at equal distances around the edge and lace with plastic clothesline, heavy cord, or shoelaces knotted together.

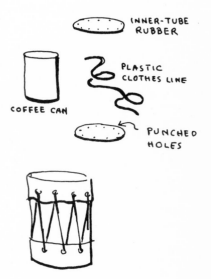

INNER-TUBE RUBBER

COFFEE CAN

PLASTIC CLOTHES LINE

PUNCHED HOLES

3. A nail keg can be used in a similar way—stretching the rubber across the open end and securing it with thumbtacks.

4. With a piece of ribbon, hang a kitchen pot by its handle around the child's neck.

Drumsticks

1. Put a wad of cotton or a small rubber ball on the end of a piece of doweling and wrap it with cloth, leatherette, chamois, or a piece of plastic or oilcloth. Secure with a rubber band or a heavy string.

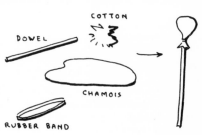

2. A ten-cent dish mop makes a good drum stick when covered with material and secured with string or a rubber band.

Jingle Bells

Jingle bells sewed to a strip of elastic are fun to wear on the wrist or around the ankles.

A Musical Instrument

From a ten-inch dowel suspend with string, individually, a tuna can, a deviled-ham can, a string of paper clips, a bell, or a spool. Tie a length of string or rope approximately fifteen inches long to each end of the dowel and use this as a handle to shake the instrument.

Woo-Woos

Blow, hum, and sputter through a cardboard tube of any length.

Streamers and Flags

Crepe-paper streamers and flags can be carried by those who do not care to participate in making music, or those who have one free hand, such as the tambourine players or rattle shakers.

AND YOU CAN DANCE TOO

Don't we look pretty when we're dancing,
  So early in the morning?

—Folk Song

AND YOU CAN DANCE TOO

Turn on the phonograph or radio, or use the Rhythm Band.

You can do circle dances, or Follow-the-Leader dances, or Free-Expression dances—everyone for himself.

You can pretend you are Bears or Tigers or Clocks or Cowboys or Popcorn Popping or Flowers Wilting or Diesel Engines, or whatever you like to be most.

And you can

skip, run, hop, walk, jump, march, leap, tiptoe, gallop, trot, stretch, sway, twirl, twist, get up, sit down, rise, fall, shake or shimmy.

And you can

Make a Conga line, do the Hokey Pokey, Skip to My Lou, dance "Farmer in the Dell," or "Ring Around the Rosy," or "London Bridge."

And you can

Help them to learn to relax, which is a useful thing to learn while they are still little. They can fall or plop on the floor

64

or sofa, and try not to move for a whole minute. Or they can lean heavily against you with all their weight, just as if they were rag dolls. Or they can take deep breaths, and then crumple, like a popped balloon.

One Word of Warning—You may think this is your great chance to dance yourself, with an appreciative audience. But some children cannot bear the sight of their parents dancing. Or sometimes they like to watch Daddy dance, but scream when Mother dances. Or they like you to dance holding them in your arms or on your feet.

DAY AFTER DAY ROUTINES

In winter I get up at night
And dress by yellow candle-light,
In summer, quite the other way,
I have to go to bed by day.

—A Child's Garden of Verses,
Robert Louis Stevenson

GETTING DRESSED

A tiny child would just as soon stay naked. Here are some things you can do, to help him change his mind.

Put your squirmy, kicking, one- to two-year-old on a high piece of furniture (hold him, naturally). The height will subdue his struggles.

Divert him by telling him funny things, or making funny faces. Play: "Where is your nose? Oh, there's your nose! Where is your tummy? Oh, there's your tummy!" This sounds elementary, but it is surprising how grim a mother can become when she engages in a dressing struggle. Don't let him think he is bothering you, if you can help it.

Buy, or make for him, loose, uncomplicated, comfortable clothes, that suit his way of life. Boxer trunks, for example, are more convenient than trunks with straps and buttons. There is nothing more harrowing than taking a well-dressed young boy to a public rest room if his costume consists of trousers that button onto straps that cross over his back, and fit into slots on his shirt, with a slipover sweater over that, and topcoat over all.

Your ultimate aim, of course, is to help him eventually to help himself. As your child grows older, it helps to <u>talk</u> the dressing, as you dress him. For example: "Now we put on your underpants, and now your undershirt, and now we pull up your trunks, and now we put on your shirt, and now we button it."

There is no point in keeping the process a mystery to him. Try to dress him in the same order each time. You can also let him fasten the last button, for practice.

It also helps to give a young child his own dressing table, even if it is an orange crate. A mirror, hung low, a brush and comb, and low hooks on which to hang clothes, all enable him to dress himself sooner, at least when he feels like it.

Design a boy (or a girl) on the floor, out of the clothes he will wear the next morning. Put his undershirt on the floor, then his top shirt over this, then his underpants underneath, then his jeans over this, then his socks under this, then his shoes under his socks. If you have a doll's or stuffed animal's head, or a coconut or orange or ball, use it for the head. And you can put a hat on this, if you want to. Then, when he awakens in the morning, there is the "boy," already to become a real boy.

Or, he can help you lay his own clothes out the night before.

It sometimes helps to mark the front of garments with a cross, mark the shoes for each foot, and fasten mittens to snow suits.

Buy boots or galoshes that are <u>easy</u> to slip on over shoes, like the ones that have zippers.

A shoehorn encourages him to put on his own shoes.

Scratch the bottom of new, slippery shoes with a knife or fork for a new walker, so he won't fall.

Put everyday clothes out where he can get to them. Put clothes you don't want him to wear, except for special occasions, out of sight, particularly if he is a Clothes Horse.

For dawdlers: If your child has to catch the nursery school bus, or make another deadline, but you just can't seem to budge him, it sometimes helps to draw a clock on a paper plate, and point out the time relationships between dressing, washing, and breakfast.

Children will dress themselves because they think it is fun to dress themselves. Don't be surprised if your child dresses himself completely, except for shoelaces, at the age of three, and at the age of four waits around for you to dress him.

THE ART OF EATING

If you're really hungry,
you'll eat your broccoli.
—Famous Folk Saying
we hope dies out

THE ART OF EATING

<u>Before they eat they have to wash their hands.</u>

"Talk it"—

"First we put the stopper in, then we turn on the cold water, (or mix it with hot if they are smart enough not to get burned), and then we reach for the soap, and then we make our hands all slippery soapy and—"

—while you wash them, and they will learn how to do it themselves.

<u>Then they sit down at the table.</u>

Sometimes parents like to eat alone, so they can talk, or have gourmet dishes, or more ceremony. Or maybe they have to, because Father gets home late. If you do eat alone, it is nice to have a family meal, once or twice a week, so the children can learn that eating is a social occasion.

If it is more convenient for the mother to feed everyone at once, but the wiggling and shifting around disturbs your digestion, you can put them at a low table near you. Low tables are more comfortable for them, anyway.

If you all eat at the same table, it helps to divide small children up between adults, so the adults can help with meat cutting, chin wiping, etc. This also prevents quarrels.

Or, as soon as the youngest child can balance a plastic plate, you can serve buffet style, sitting down at the table to eat. Buffet style is an easy way for the mother to serve. Or the father can serve while the mother finishes in the kitchen. The children can indicate how much of each dish they want. And they can learn to help themselves to second helpings.

In good weather, the patio or yard off the kitchen or a back porch is a nice and practical place to give them their meals.

You can vary things for them, especially at lunch time. They can eat outdoors, or you can pack a picnic lunch for them and put it in their wagon and let them find their own picnic spot in the backyard. Show them how to put the scraps back into their wagon when they are finished.

Little children like lunch boxes or bag lunches, just like the school children have.

Invite guests for your children from time to time. What is nice about this is that they may get invited to the guest's home in return.

If tempers are frayed at lunch time, or the children become too excited just before naps, you can invite guests for an early supper instead.

Plastic table mats inspire neatness.

Salad forks are good in-between forks.

A flower, or centerpiece made out of small toys, such as ducks on a mirror, is fun.

Let them practice cutting soft food, such as waffles, with a knife and fork.

If children grow restless, they can help clear the dishes between courses.

Always give them small helpings at first, and let them ask for more.

A sponge is handy to have near at hand for messy eaters. You can also put oilcloth or newspapers under their chairs.

If you are eating with them, and do not serve buffet, or they are not old enough to help themselves, tell them you will pass out the second helpings all at once, when you are finished with your first helping.

Children can learn to pour from a small pitcher by putting one hand on the handle and one hand on the front of the pitcher.

Children like to help plan the menu occasionally, or make a special dish, such as Jello, for dessert. They can also help set the table. Even a two-year-old can put the napkins around.

Children like to know where food comes from—the details of the journey from farm to table.

If mealtimes are quarrelsome, it sometimes helps to play records while children eat.

If your children arise in the morning in a grumpy mood, it is often wise to postpone breakfast rather than give them a marvelous opportunity to throw or spill food, or simply refuse to eat.

Mothers sometimes greet little children returning home from nursery school at noontime by saying, "Lunch is ready." But often they have to have a while to roam about and become used to the transition. If you are having trouble with lunch, after nursery school, it is often a good idea to wait awhile, even though their being in nursery school gave you a chance to have lunch all ready.

If a certain meal, such as breakfast, is particularly horrible, you might talk this over with a child who is old enough to understand. He might suggest that breakfast would be more pleasant if he had cereal, instead of eggs, or if you laid out the breakfast food on the counter, and let him help himself.

When you eat with them, have simple pleasant conversation, and save the passionate discussions of a new house or job for later.

An occasional trip to a restaurant is fun, and good training, too. Choose a restaurant that welcomes children. Don't go in the rush hours, when service may be slow. (See "How to Order for Children" under Traveling with Little Children.)

True Anecdotes

We know a family with five children whose mealtimes were chaotic. The father, who had a scientific bent of mind, decided to take a wire recording of dinner one evening, and see where the trouble lay.

After dinner they sat down and played the record back. Amidst the confusion, with everyone talking, a polite, tiny voice said, "Please pass the butter." Everyone went on talking and paid no attention. The polite tiny voice said again, a bit louder, "Please pass the butter!" Everyone went on talking. Then the voice said, still louder, and not so politely, "Pass the butter!" Everyone went on talking. Then the voice shrieked at the top of its lungs, "I want the butter!" Immediately, both parents cried, "If you're going to talk like that, you can leave the table at once!"

MORAL: You have to listen, at least some of the time.

In another family, whose two children sat at a small table, there was a squabble every mealtime over who got the red chair and who got the yellow chair. The red chair was the most desirable. Whoever sat in the red chair was able to eat happily. Whoever sat in the yellow chair threw his food and refused to eat.

Getting another red chair seemed expensive, but perhaps sensible. But then they might fight over the new red chair. Suggesting that they take turns had no effect, as their memory spans were too short.

One day the father was officiating at the meal when the squabble broke out. He took a shirt cardboard and made a chart with both of their names, and pinned the chart on the wall over their table. Though they could not read, the chart seemed impressive. The father drew a tiny red chair with a red crayon, and a tiny yellow chair with a yellow crayon, under their names. At the next meal, this was reversed. The chart seemed to have an intrinsic power of its own. The chart was Law and Order and Authority.

They would not eat sweet potatoes. And they would not eat anything else if the sweet potatoes were on their plates. Just to look at a sweet potato was loathsome. Then the mother stuck a date on a toothpick and stuck the toothpick in a sweet potato for a flag, and this made the sweet potato a boat. And they were very happy to have boats on their plates. But they would not eat their boats. In fact, they would not eat anything else, either, because they were too busy pushing their boats all over their plates, and dumping the other food in the boats for cargo. And so there isn't any moral to this, except maybe it's better not to eat a boat than not to eat a sweet potato.

At dinner, the children squirmed, squealed, quarreled and interrupted. They reached for things across the table instead of asking for them, please, and they got up and wandered off in the middle of the meal, and they kicked their chair legs and leaned back in their chairs, and if, by chance, they were served something they didn't like, they screamed it was Icky.

Father and Mother found themselves joining in the fray, also screaming, and often threatening.

And then they had an idea. Once a week was Formal Dinner. The two little boys wore Daddy's ties, over their T-shirts, and the little girl wore Mother's old high heels. And there was candlelight and soft music on the radio, and place cards at each place.

Father changed into his old clothes after dinner, instead of before. The first time, Mother was so busy, she just came in her shorts as usual, until the children complained she was not dressed up, too. So she went into her bedroom and put on a dress, and all the shiny, rhinestone jewelry she could find. And when she came back, Father stood up, and the boys stood up, and Father held her chair for her, and everyone had the best of manners. During dinner, Father and Mother searched their memories for stories of Grand Banquets they had attended, or pretended they had attended.

And a little of the Good Behavior at the Formal Dinner rubbed off at the informal dinners during the rest of the week. And when the Good Behavior was practically gone, they had another Formal Dinner.

BATH TIME

Clean, oh, clean, yes, clean, oh, clean.
Clean, oh, clean, yes, clean, oh, clean.
Scrubbity, scrubbity, rubby dub dubbity
And make me nice and clean-o.

—Woody Guthrie

BATH TIME

There is a lot more to a bath besides just getting clean. It can also be a physical and spiritual revival.

Put a rubber mat down in the tub, so children won't slip. Then sit down in the bathroom, with a book, or newspaper, or sewing, while they play. Water play is so engrossing for them, it can be your chance to relax.

Here are some things that are especially fun to play with in the bathtub:

Funnels, strainers, egg beaters, pots and pans, straws to blow through, tiny boats, and whatever else they may drag in.

Paint brushes to paint the side of the bathtub with soap

Bubble bath and colored vegetable water to liven things up.

A spray hose, the kind you use for washing your hair, attached to the spigot, makes a tiny shower.

Bubble pipes.

They can wear their bathing suits, sometimes. And you can even help them to practice swimming.

It is a good time to cut fingernails.

And they can even learn to wash and dry themselves, too.

If you make the bath so enjoyable that they don't want to get out, say: "We will let the water out first. When it goes glug-glug, it's time to climb out."

SOME GOOD WAYS TO GO NIGHT NIGHT

Rock-a-Bye baby, thy cradle is green,
Father's a nobleman, mother's a queen;
And Betty's a lady, and wears a gold ring,
And Johnny's a drummer, and drums for the king.

—Old Lullaby

NIGHT NIGHT

We would like to repeat what we said in our preface, here. Don't try all of these ideas. And they certainly aren't for settling any special bedtime problem. They are just for fun.

For Babies

Find a magazine. Settle the baby on your lap, turn the pages, and point out the different pictures, saying, "The airplane goes Night Night," "The Cadillac goes Night Night," "The beautiful lady with the nice smile goes Night Night," "The cigarettes go Night Night," "The tomato soup goes Night Night," until the baby is mesmerized and begins to nod—and then you say, "The baby goes Night Night," and pick him up, and put him in his crib.

Put on some dreamy music and hold the baby in your arms and dance dreamily, and, as the music ends, dance him into his bed. If the baby can walk, you might have a special Night Night tune, such as "Pomp and Circumstance," by which you march to bed with ceremony.

Older Children

If you have a time clock, set it for ten minutes and say, "When the buzzer rings, it's bedtime." A buzzer has an impersonal authority which a parent often lacks.

Old school yells, such as "Give 'Em the Axe," or "Rickety Rack," done in action, while not soothing the children, are often diverting enough to make them a quiet audience before lights out.

Sometimes it is fun to go to bed backwards, or crawling on your hands and knees or walking blindfolded, or swimming on the floor, or to be carried in on a chair.

72

If your child does not like his bed, maybe he would like to sleep under it, or in a corner, as long as it is in his room. However, if you feel that the place to go to bed is bed, there is nothing wrong with your attitude.

> Letting a child play for a long, relaxed time in a lukewarm bath is very soporific. If he should be watched, it is a good time for you to read the evening paper. (See Bathtime)

Take the child out of doors, or hold him up to a window, and let him say good night to everything he can see.

"Good night Moon, good night Stars, good night Fence, good night Wheelbarrow, goodnight my rubber boots, good night Elm Tree."

This may be topped off by, "Good night, Johnny."

> If your child has just visited his grandparents or gone to a restaurant, and is so excited he can't sleep, tell him the story of what just happened, so it will take on some order in his mind. Tell it very quietly, as if out of a book.

There are different ways to read a good book to the children. You can read it to them, or tell them the story that goes with the pictures, or let them tell it with you. It's better to pick a short story or some poems than to hurry through a long one, turning the pages before they are through looking at the pictures. And you can say, "Tonight it's Martha's turn to choose a story, and tomorrow night it will be Peter's turn."

No fair German Lieder!

Sometimes you get tired of reading (especially when one of the children is too young to understand the words and just wants to grab the book). So you can sing songs, instead.

A version of "Good Night Ladies," substituting your children's names, is a good finale.

Singing in front of the fire is a special, cozy treat.

Children like songs with lots of repetition like, "Come, Come, Come, Come to the Church in the Wildwood," or "The Bear Went Over the Mountain," or whatever is in your repertoire.

This is also an excellent opportunity to have an audience for your voice.

You can <u>draw</u> stories, too, if you can draw at all.

"Once upon a time there was a little girl, and her name was Rosalind, and one day her mother and daddy said to her, 'Rosalind, you are old enough to eat in a restaurant if you have good manners', and she said, 'I will have very good manners, oh, I promise"—and so—etc.

The Gradual Transition Method: Dress them for bed. Then they can have ten minutes more to play in the living room, ten minutes to play in their room, and five minutes in bed with the light on. Then, lights out!

Some children like to put their doll or Teddy to bed first.

An adaptation of the Reed Method is very soothing. Deep breaths, a back rub, a monotonous, calm voice, and saying, "Now the eyebrows are going to sleep, now the nose is going to sleep, now the chin is going to sleep, etc."

Counting "One, to get off the sofa,
Two, to take off your clothes,
Three, to put on your pajamas,
Four, to brush your teeth,
Five, to pop into bed."

If you have lots of children, special Late Privileges for one child at a time gives each child a chance to be alone with his parents, which they like.

Talk about Today, and what happened that was nice. And talk about Tomorrow, and what will be fun.

FINGER PLAYS

Here are mother's knives and forks
Here is mother's table.
Here is sister's looking glass
Here is baby's cradle.

Most of the finger plays listed here are done to the words of time-worn ditties which have been passed down from generation to generation. They are still diverting to little children, appealing as they do to their sense of rhythm and of riddles, or make-believe and action.

1. I'm a little teapot, short and stout

    Here is my handle   (right hand on hip)

    Here is my spout   (bend left elbow, with hand and fingers pointing away from body)

    When I get all steamed up, then I shout

    Tip me over, pour me out!   (bend body from the waist to the left)

2. Little tiny ball   (make circle with thumb and index finger)

    Middle-sized ball   (make circle with hands, fingers touching)

    Great big ball   (make circle with hands and arms, fingers touching above the head)

3. Two little blackbirds, sitting on a hill   (hands closed, thumbs up)

    One named Jack, one named Jill   (wiggle one thumb, then wiggle the other thumb)

    Fly away, Jack, fly away, Jill   (put hand behind back, then other hand behind back)

    Come back, Jack, come back, Jill.   (return hands, one at a time, with thumb up)

75

4. Jack be nimble

   Jack be quick

   (thumb of left hand is extended, and index and middle finger of right hand walk over to thumb and jump over it)

   Jack jump over the candle-stick.

5. One little, two little, three little Indians
   Four little, five little, six little Indians
   Seven little, eight little, nine little Indians
   Ten little Indian boys.

   (starting with fists clenched, extend one finger at a time)

6. (To the tune of Frere Jacques)

   Where is Thumpkin?   (hands closed, right thumb up)

   Where is Thumpkin?

   Here I am!   (raise left thumb, and wiggle)

   Here I am!

   How are you today, sir?   (raise right thumb, and wiggle)

   Very well, I thank you.   (wiggle left thumb)

   Run away, run away.   (hide thumbs in hand)

7. These are spyglasses   (make circle out of fingers around the eyes)

   This is my new red cap   (place hands on top of head)

   This is the way we fold our hands   (fold)

   And put them in our lap.   (place)

8. Here is a beehive. Where are the bees?   (one hand closed)

   Hidden away where nobody sees.

   Soon they come creeping out of the hive.

   One, two, three, four, five.   (extend one finger at a time)

9. It's a very rainy day
   And I can't go out to play

So Mother into her basket slipped
And found some scissors,

(cup left hand for imaginary basket and dip right hand into basket and snip with index and <u>middle fingers</u>)

Snip, snip, snip.

10. Open, shut them, open, shut them,

(both hands open, both hands clenched, open, clenched)

Give a little clap.

(clap)

Open, shut them, open, shut them,

(hands open, hands clenched)

Lay them in your lap.

(place in lap)

11. Planting seeds: A ditty for planting seeds, or it can be a counting game using one hand.

One for the blackbird
One for the crow,
One for the cutworm
And two to grow!

(extend fingers, one at a time)

12. Here is the church

(palms together, fingers laced)

Here is the steeple.

(point index fingers up)

Open the doors,
Where are the people?

(spread thumbs)
(turn palms upward)

Here is the church

(put backs of hands together, lace fingers next to palms)

Here is the steeple
Open the doors,
Here are all the people!

(point index fingers up)
(thumbs spread)
(wiggle fingers)

13. Here are Mother's knives and forks

(put backs of hands together, lace fingers next to palms, palms up)

Here is Mother's table.

(turn palms down, fingers still interlaced)

Here is Sister's looking glass

(index fingers make a point)

Here is Baby's cradle.

(little fingers up like index fingers and rock hands)

14. Knock at the door
Peek in

(forehead)
(eyes)

Turn the knob   (nose)
And walk in   (mouth)

Chin chopper, chin chopper,   (chin)
chin, chin, chin.

15. Here sits the Lord Mayor   (forehead)
Here sit his two men   (eyes)
Here sits the cock   (right cheek)
Here sits the hen   (Left cheek)
Here sit the chickens   (nose)
And here they run in   (mouth)
Chin chopper, chin chopper,   (chin)
chin, chin, chin.

16. If you lived up here   (forehead)
And I lived down there   (chin)
I wouldn't   go all the way   (finger goes around side of face,
around this way to see you   from chin to forehead)

Or this way   (other side of face)

I'd just go up like that!   (straight up from chin to forehead, fast)

17. Adam and Eve and Pinch Me
Went down to the river to
bathe
Adam and Eve were drowned
Who do you think was saved?   (Answer is Pinch Me, and you
do)

18. (When child's feet are bare)
Shoe the old horse, shoe the
old mare,
But let the little colt go bare,
bare, bare   (pat the bottom of feet)

19. (For bare toes)
This little pig went to market
This little pig stayed home
This little pig had roast beef
This little pig had none
This little pig cried, "wee,   (from big toe to little toe)
wee, wee," all the way home.

or

20. This little one eats grass
This little one eats hay
This little one drinks water
This little one runs away
This little one does nothing,
But lie around all day.   (from big toe to little toe)

21. (For fathers, or mothers with strong leg muscles: place child across your foot)

Ride a cock horse to Banbury Cross
To see a fine lady upon a fine horse

With rings on her fingers and bells on her toes

She shall have music where-ever she goes.

22. (For a ride on the knees)

Trot, trot to Boston
Trot, trot to Lynn
Trot, trot to Salem
Then trot home again.

or

23. Trot, trot to Boston
To buy a fat pig
Home again, home again
Jiggity, jig.   (the whole verse slowly)

Trot, trot to Boston
To buy a fat hog
Home again, home again
Jiggity, jog.   (second verse very slowly)

24. (Another ride on the knees)

This is the way the lady rides
Trot - Trot - Trot   (gently)
This is the way the gentle-man rides
Gallop - Gallop - Gallop   (stately)
This is the way the farmer rides
Hobble-de-hoy - Hobble-de-hoy   (rolling from side to side)

25. Hand tower   (build the tower with two or more children by alternating hands. The hand on the bottom of the table goes to the top of the pile and so on)

26. Eeensie Weensie Spider

Went up the waterspout

(index finger and thumb from opposite hands crawl up an imaginary wall)

Down came the rain and washed the spider out

(both hands extended above head come down slowly, fingers wiggling)

Out came the sun and dried away the rain

(big circle with arms above head, fingers touching)

And the Eeensie Weensie Spider

Went up the spout again.

(index finger and thumb from opposite hand crawl up wall)

OTHER THINGS THAT HAPPEN

Hippity hop to the barber shop
To get a stick of candy!

—Nursery Rhyme

HAIRCUTS

At the Barber Shop:

Haircuts can be frightening, because most barbers wear white coats just like doctors who give shots. And the clippers make a scary sound. And anyway, who likes to have his head fooled with in this way?

But there are some things you might do.

Go by a barber shop. Look in the window. Let him watch Daddy get a haircut. Let her watch Mother. Just before you take him, act it out. Pretend you have clippers and go Buzz all over his head.

Sometimes a child wants his mother to sit in the barber chair and hold him in her lap.

At Home:

Buy your own equipment and do it yourself. If your children behave better for other people, make it a Neighborhood Haircutting Session, and all the neighborhood children can have their hair cut at the same time, like a party.

Give everyone a sheet, or take turns with the sheet. Let them hold a comb and mirror, just like at the real barber's. Brush their necks with talcum and put some sweet-smelling stuff on their hair. Then have ice cream.

Sometimes a little child can be diverted while having his hair cut by setting him in front of the dishwasher, while it runs, or the TV set or the dryer. If he isn't diverted by the machinery in your house any more, try a neighbor's.

You can cut his hair before his bath, so the bath will wash off the "tickles."

CHILDREN HELP

And what about Johnny? He split the kindling,
filled the woodbox, lugged the water, fed the creatures,
fished the brook, and whistled at his work.

—Journey Cake, Ho!
Ruth Sawyer

CHILDREN HELP

Few children care if the house is neat and tidy, but they do like to play "Grownup." Grownups work, so it is natural that children will play Work. They especially like to play Work if they can do the same thing mother is doing, or if she is not more than a few feet away.

If they are looking for approval, they will get it here. The smallest task such as handing Mommy a spoon is usually received with the most enthusiastic appreciation. But praise for stirring batter in a bowl and blame for stirring mud in the flower bed sometimes may seem puzzling to a child.

Children like to perform prodigious tasks and will do them several minutes at a time or several days in a row, and then may stop, right in the middle of the job. If they are playing Mud Pies and quit, you don't care. But somehow, when they are playing Work, you may think they ought to finish what they started.

Here are some things that some of the children do some of the time, but none of the children do all of the time:

Emptying the waste baskets:
If you find the child can empty the waste basket into the trash burner successfully, but has a hard time getting it back in the house in the proper place, make an X mark with chalk on the floor or rug where it belongs.

Setting the table:
>Anything that isn't too hot or too heavy children can manage to get on the table. and don't usually object to some necessary rearranging on your part.

Bringing in the newspaper or mail:
>It doesn't usually occur to parents that this is a good idea until the child has presented you with all the papers he could carry from neighboring porches.

Sorting the laundry:
>Fun and easy. White clothes go in this pile, all others in this pile.

Hanging clothes:
>A child that will hand you wet clothes from the basket can really save your back. "Daddy's shirt, Mommy's slip, my pants," is the game which accompanies this activity.

Dusting:
>Children can wear men's socks on their hands and dust table tops and rungs of chairs.

Dish washing:
>If you are concerned about your best china, wash it first. Then invite the child to help with the silver, plastics, and iron wear. A game called "pouring" is very popular with preschoolers. The child stands at the kitchen sink and pours water from one container to another.

Vacuuming:
>A child cannot possibly clean your house or even a room completely, but he can work over the middle of the living-room carpet, a chair, or an area of bare floor.

Watering house plants:
>If the pots or containers are small enough to carry to the kitchen sink, this is safest. Let the child fill a small can with water, then slowly pour it on the plants.

Cleaning fish and turtle bowls; bird cages:
>Once the animal is removed, there's no reason to be nervous.

Shining shoes for the family:
>Shoe polish and small children have never been a good combination. But some children will work fiendishly getting a high shine with a brush or cloth, after you have applied the polish.

Carrying wood and laying the fire:
>This is a job children fight over.

Caring for animals:
>Children can feed, water, and walk the dog, or let the cats in the house in the morning.

Putting groceries away:

Oranges in the bin, cleanser under the sink, paper napkins in the drawer, canned goods in the pantry, soap in the bathroom.

Washing windows:

Wiping a wet sponge across a bar of Bon-Ami and applying it to windows is fun for a while. When picture making with fingers takes over, don't discourage it. It all wipes off with a clean cloth.

Polishing floors:

Sliding on freshly waxed floors in clean socks or being pulled on scatter rugs is a treat for both the child and the floor.

Outdoor Helpers

Rake leaves and grass clippings.
Sweep porches and steps.
Help Daddy wash the car with big sponges.
Water grass with a hose.
Hose screens and windows.

Often children volunteer their services in answering the phone. Whether they talk or just breathe heavily, they rarely get the message. Others like to bring in heavy, slippery milk bottles from off the porch. Other "helpers" like to "ride" the vacuum while you are running it or get in or on the bed while you are making it. Playing games such as "You pretend you're asleep in this bed, and I'll pretend to make sister's bed," do not always work, nor does it always work to make the beds together. Sometimes the beds never get made.

It is often easier to do the work yourself, but turning work into play is part of their growing up.

WHEN COMPANY COMES

Little children should be seen and not heard.

—Old Folk Saying

WHEN COMPANY COMES

Sometimes, when company comes, little children act particularly bad. Then you have to say, "I don't know what has got into them. They aren't like this, ordinarily." And the company doesn't believe you.

Probably the reason they are acting worse than usual is that they sense you want them to put on a special little show. And they don't know why. And this upsets them. Or maybe you are so glad to see the company, they are jealous. Or maybe company just excites them, and they go crazy.

Here are some ways to help them:

If you know you are going to have company beforehand, tell them who is coming, and what will happen, and just how long they may stay up. Maybe the company will come in and say good night to them.

Children can help by being "extra hosts" and passing the refreshments. You can tell them beforehand to wait for their turn before they help themselves.

You can give them their own hors d'oeuvres plate and when they are finished, it is bedtime.

Get your children into their night clothes before the company comes. And put them to bed before they become too excited.

As a special treat you can skip the afternoon nap, if your child does not become terribly overtired. Then you can draw a clock face under his clock, and say, "When this time comes, it is your bedtime."

If you are having a large party, and want the children out of the way for part of it, you might hire a sitter, whom they know, to read or play with them in their room. Sometimes an older child is more appealing.

If it is going to be a very large, noisy party, the child could spend the night at the sitter's house.

Sometimes it helps to have a special toy, like a new record, to bring out when company comes—not as a bribe, but as a special treat.

If children are coming with the company, you might set up a separate, children's party in your child's room—graham crackers or popcorn, and juice in an unbreakable easy-to-pour pitcher with unbreakable glasses. Tell your child he is going to be host or hostess, just like you are. Teach him how to pass the crackers and pour the juice.

It is often extremely helpful to act out a situation before it occurs. Or even afterwards, for the next time. Tell them you like to talk to your friends, the same way they like to talk and play with their friends. Then pretend the doorbell is ringing, or make one child the company and he can ring the doorbell. Another child can answer the door, and say, "Please come in and sit down." Then that child can talk to the company for a while. He can say, "I'm three and a half years old, and I'm going to have a birthday and I'm going to get an Indian suit."

And the company can say, "Isn't that nice!" Then the child must find something to do. If it is a very quiet thing, he can do it in the same room with the company. If it is a noisy thing, he can do it outside or in his room. Pretty soon it is time for the company to leave, and then the child can say good-by. After that he can yell or run up and down if he feels like it.

NEIGHBORHOOD PLAY

Of all the pestilences dire,
Including famine, flood and fire,
By Satan and his imps rehearsed,
The neighbor's children are the worst.

—Philosophy for Parents
Stoddard King

NEIGHBORHOOD PLAY

When your child begins to play in his neighborhood, you will find yourself a part of a new society, too.

There will be War and Peace, Love and Hate, Comedy and Tragedy.

When you pass out crackers, a whole box may suddenly disappear.

A strange child will wander in to use the toilet, while you are taking a bath.

A battle may rage in your petunia bed. Faces may study you over the fence, or through knotholes, while you are giving a barbecue party in your back yard.

And, with any group of human beings (especially between the ages of one and five), there will be personality problems:

Robert Johnson, who walks off with everything that isn't nailed down.

Annie Burke, who lives at your house because her mother works, or has new twins, or plays bridge all afternoon.

William Pennington, whom your child idolizes and copies and quotes, so that it seems you are living with William, instead of your own "well-brought-up" little boy.

The Big Boy who pushes, or the Little Boy whom your child dominates.

Maybe you wish your child hadn't made his debut. Maybe you wish he was still behind the fence, unexposed to the ways of the world.

But you can also consider this a part of your own and your child's education. It will give you a perspective on your own children, give your child companions, and provide him with a microcosm of what is to come in school and the outside world.

Of course you will want to carry on your own standards.

You might try:

> Telling Robert calmly and sweetly that he may play with the toy truck at your house whenever he wants to, but please leave it here. You don't have to frisk him whenever he walks out of your house, but you can keep an eye on him, knowing his particular habit.

> As for Annie Burke—your house is just more fun. If you don't want your children to play at her house, completely unsupervised, keep them busy and happy at home. There is usually an Annie Burke orphan in every neighborhood.

> William Pennington represents something wonderful to your child. It is probably just part of his growing process, and doesn't mean William Pennington has any Svengali powers. You might point out to your little boy that he doesn't have to do everything William's way—that he has his own good ideas, too.

> The Big Boy who pushes, or takes over your children's toys, probably gets pushed around in his own age group, for some reason. As long as you are sure your child isn't provoking him unnecessarily, you might lay down a firm rule—if he wants to play in your yard, he must not push, and must take turns with the toys. (There is an age between one and three when children often push.)

> If your child is the bossy one, you might try to find older children for him to play with, and give him lots of confidence in himself at the same time.

If one friendship is excluding all others, and neither child seems to be benefiting, you might try inviting other children over, or for a ride to the grocery store. But there may be something wonderful about the best friend that will be missed.

Around the age of four, children form "cliques" and gang up on others. As long as this is reversed often enough, and your child is not always the butt or the aggressor, you may consider it part of growing up.

86

It is a good idea to be around without "hovering" over them, to suggest new activities or diversions.

Sample Situation:

Fight over toy train:

Your child is complaining that William Pennington is touching it, and he is the only one who is supposed to. Your child picks up a hammer. Mother steps in, takes hammer. ("You don't hit with things, ever.")

Mother: Wait a moment, now tell me—where is the train going? Is it going to San Francisco?

Children are silent. Fight stops. Mother has time to think fast.

Mother: Is it going to San Francisco or Los Angeles?

Child: Los Angeles.

Mother: Well, if it is going to Los Angeles it has to go through a tunnel, and you don't have a tunnel, so one of you can build a tunnel out of blocks and the other one can run the train through it.

Or she might suggest juice and crackers on the terrace, so they forget the train. Or a trip to the grocery store. And if she thinks her own child is overtired and ripe for a quarrel, she might read to them for a few moments, and then William Pennington can go home and come back after naps.

If you feel your child is not playing "creatively" enough of the time, but just wanders up and down the street aimlessly with the gang, a good nursery school may help. If a nursery school is not available, or is too expensive, many mothers have organized co-operative play groups, which have their good and bad sides.

Co-operative Play Group

A co-operative play group is made up of three to six mothers with children of the same preschool age. It depends upon the child, but two and a half is almost always the earliest age that a child derives benefit. Mixed ages, as three-year-olds in with four-and-a-half-year-olds, present special problems as the stages are so different. On the other hand, it is more like a real family situation. It is nice to divide the sexes as evenly as possible. And what is most important is to find mothers who share your same ideas and enthusiasm and willingness to work.

If one mother is shocked and cannot hide her feelings that a three-year-old is not completely toilet trained, if one mother feels children should be severely disciplined if they ever hit, if another mother puts tidiness at the top of her list of virtues, the children will become confused from inconsistent handling. A bad nursery school or play group is worse than none at all.

You will have to get together for discussion, and you will have to set up the best physical environment that you can. If you are going to buy or build any equipment, one mother can have swings, one a jungle gym, and another a large sand pile, etc. If one yard is set up better than the others, you might always have the school there, three times a week, and relieve that mother from other duties. As few different places as possible is better for the children anyway.

Here are some suggestions which are useful for handling one child, as well as a large group of children:

1. Don't force your child to stay in a strange yard without you. Stay with him until he feels comfortable. Eventually he will notice that the other children get along without their mothers, and will let you go. When you do go, tell him you are going, and when you will return.

2. Don't shout directions to children into the air. Speak in a low, natural voice, directly to the child. Don't talk baby talk. Expect them to do what you want, but don't want too much.

3. Be on guard for fatigue symptoms, and act accordingly. Suggest a quieter activity, such as reading to them.

4. Provide enough equipment, and keep it in good repair. (See Outdoor Play Equipment.)

5. In giving directions, say, "It's time to wash your hands," rather than, "Do you want to wash your hands?" or, "Come wash your hands!"

6. Give a child time enough to finish his project before he must leave it, by warning him it is almost time for juice and crackers, so he had better get the truck into the garage, etc.

7. If Dickie has been on the swing for a long time, and Sally wants it, tell Sally you will help her ask Dickie for a turn, and carry through until you get the swing.

8. If a child is playing house and complains, "They won't let me play," suggest to the child that he knock on the playhouse door and tell them he has come to pay a visit.

9. Don't ask them what they want to do, if there is no real choice.

10. Saying, "Feet belong on the floor," often works better than, "Do not walk on the table."

11. Give a child the help he needs, but no more than he needs.

12. If one child starts screaming (for joy), and is joined by eight more, pretend you are enjoying it, and then suggest that everyone be as quiet as they can, and just whisper.

A very good book on organizing a playgroup: A Playgroup Handbook for Parents and Leaders by Lovisa C. Wagoner, published by Olympic College, Bremerton, Washington. Price: $1.50. This covers the health and economic side of such a project, and gives you many useful suggestions for guiding the children at play.

In many residential neighborhoods you must get the permission of your neighbors and the Planning Commission of your community in order to organize such a group.

We have known of some mothers who get together and hire an outside person to be the supervisor. But it has to be absolutely the right person. If you find such a person, however, the children may benefit from being guided by one adult, rather than many different ones.

Here are some other ideas we have received from parents who live in neighborhoods:

1. Organize a Halloween party or Easter Parade.

2. Get together and put up street signs that warn drivers to go slowly because children are playing.

3. Get together and block off part of a street for play.

4. Buy a vacant lot for playground equipment with a group of neighbors.

5. If you have a congenial neighbor with children the same age, have a gate that opens into the next yard, or take down the fence for a larger play area.

6. Organize a reading group, or Sunday School.

7. One neighborhood group even built a swimming pool, and hired a professional lifeguard to be on duty.

8. Take turns with your neighbors inviting children to lunch or taking them to a playground.

9. A Co-op Sitter Service. (See Sitters)

A neighborhood is an exciting place for a child. There is nothing more thrilling than digging in a vacant lot, having fences to climb, even feuds and romances.

Just as long as an imaginative and intelligent adult is in the background.

And when you complain that you are one of the few mothers who bother or care about what is going on—remember that being imaginative and intelligent is always work.

DOCTOR'S ORDERS

They expounded the reazels
For sneezles
And wheezles,
The manner of measles
When new
They said, "If he freezles
In draughts and in breezles,
Then phtheezles
May even ensue."

—Now We Are Six
A. A. Milne

DOCTOR'S ORDERS

(If you have a child who asks for his medicine and takes his nose drops without complaining, you can skip this chapter and worry about his becoming a hypochondriac.)

We think that Firmness plus a Casual Approach is the best theory, here. But there are still useful tricks for carrying out Doctor's Orders that make them less grim for you and the child. If you tried all of these suggestions, you would certainly lose face, but a few of them may help avoid a battle which you will win only because you are physically stronger.

Medicine

If you have to give nose drops, baby aspirin, an antibiotic, and take temperatures every four hours, try to schedule them so that they will all come at the same time. Then you don't have to poke and prod him every hour. If this is impossible, and you are forgetful, keep a chart so you remember when something is due.

Prepare everything first before you present it, so that you are not dashing about for a glass of water, holding a spoonful of medicine in your hand.

A tray, with the medicine, water and perhaps a flower or special treat, is a pleasant, ceremonious way to present the medicine.

If the dose is a teaspoon, try giving him a half teaspoon, then the other half, and you will avoid spilling and be certain all of it goes down.

A funnel or nose dropper or straw is another way of avoiding spills. You might give him a choice—shall we put it in a funnel or a spoon?

Some children enjoy taking the medicine themselves. This naturally takes longer, but gives them pride. You have to watch, of course, to see that they don't pour it down the sink.

Again—the kitchen clock. When the buzzer rings, it's Medicine Time.

If you can combine the medicine with food, don't use a food he is only lukewarm about. If he doesn't finish it, you are not sure how much of the medicine he took. Make a point of having ice cream or pudding, or whatever his favorite food is, in the house.

After applying the sting-y medicine to a cut you can draw a baby or a moon on his knee with the medicine for a treat. Or you can let him put on his own Band-Aid. Or give him an extra Band-Aid for himself or his Teddy.

You can make up a Medicine Song, or count, "One, Two, Three, Bottoms Up!" Or shut your eyes, and ask him to tell you when it's all gone, so you can open them.

If it is liquid medicine, and you can use vegetable coloring, you can ask him what color he wants his medicine this time—green, pink, blue, etc.

You can dramatize the situation, and pretend you are the nurse or doctor, and he is your patient.

One pediatric nurse we talked to carries the glass of medicine to a patient, sets it down casually, and talks to the patient. She says the child usually reaches for it, and drains it. If he does not, she offers it herself, still casually, which usually works.

An old-fashioned but good method: Tell him to hold his nose, and he will open his mouth.

Nose Drops

If you have a young child who cannot be reasoned with, you can wrap him up in a sheet, like a strait jacket. This may sound like torture, but it is actually better than sitting on his stomach, holding his arms, and poking him with the dropper when he wiggles.

An older child enjoys a game or silly rhyme while he holds his head down and waits for the drops to sink in.

Soaking Hands and Feet

If you have to soak a hurt or swollen limb for a certain time, and the child grows impatient, try putting marbles in the bottom of the washbowl or dish, which he can finger. Also, start out by making the water lukewarm, and then getting it gradually hotter.

Casts

Put a cast on a doll.

Tell neighborhood children that the child will appear in odd apparatus. Ask them in for cast-drawing party.

Exercises

Do them yourself with the child, to music.

Glasses

Become familiar with the idea of glasses, first.

Get everyone "play" glasses in family and say, "You have the only real ones."

Make a child's glasses case out of felt and sequins. Have a special place to put glasses at night.

Let child have some choice in glasses' frames.

Shots

Tell them to say, "Ouch!" first—or to hold their nose.

An older child can learn to stand on one leg, and relax the opposite hip where the shot goes. It hurts less.

At the Doctor's Office

If you think you may have to wait a long time, plan to use the time to advantage. There are so few times during the day when a mother is free just to read or talk to her children. Take along a good book, one that you have wanted to read to them, or take paper and pencil and draw pictures. If you know they are going to have a shot, you can draw a picture of a boy or girl having a shot. This may take some of the fear out of it for them.

Dentists

Let your child watch you sometime at the dentist's, when you are just getting your teeth cleaned. Then he will become familiar with the weird apparatus, and the strange noises. When he goes for a filling, don't tell him it won't hurt.

Hospitals

If possible, drive your child to the hospital some day, before he goes, and let him see what it looks like. Tell him everything that will happen to him in as much detail as possible. There are books, such as <u>Linda Goes to the Hospital,</u> which are also helpful. Again, tell him when it will hurt, but also point out the interesting part of it to him. When you visit him in the hospital and the time comes to leave, you might say, "In ten minutes the nurses are going to kick us out, but we will be back to take you home tomorrow morning." If this is the case.

In all sicknesses, stress the "getting well" part of it, rather than the "sick" part. Don't say, "If you don't take your medicine, you won't get well." But explain to him how the medicine is helping him to get well, so he can soon go outside and play again.

STAY-IN-BED DAYS

When I was sick and lay a-bed,
I had two pillows at my head,
And all my toys beside me lay
To keep me happy all the day.

—<u>A Child's Garden of Verses,</u>
Robert Louis Stevenson

STAY-IN-BED DAYS

It is easier to keep a child in bed if all of the <u>Things</u> are with him.

1. A mesh bag in which potatoes come from the grocery store can be pinned to the mattress; his toys are then within easy reach.

2. A shoe bag can be hung from the bed or on the wall next to the bed—one compartment for his slippers, the others for his treasures.

Sick people like to be pampered. Children are like people.

1. Surround him with pillows from <u>your</u> bed. A little girl will feel cozy in <u>your</u> bed jacket.

2. If the illness does not last long enough for friends and relatives to send "get-well-quick" cards, Daddy could mail a picture postcard of his office building or of the hotel where he eats lunch.

3. Daddy might call during the lunch hour to see how "the patient" is doing.

4. Decorate his bed tray with flowers.
Cut his toast into squares, circles, triangles, or strips.

Cut his orange into fourth's or eighth's, or separate it like the petals of a flower.

Float a peapod boat on his tomato soup (very simply made by forcing open the pod with a length of toothpick).

Tuck a small new toy, like a harmonica, under his napkin, or under his plate turned upside down.

Bed patients like straws and toothpicks.

Have a surprise tray. Wrap the food in separate paper bags and have the patient guess what's for lunch by feeling and smelling the bags.

If his appetite is lagging, put food on skewers. Good skewer foods are green beans, pineapple chunks, or bit sizes of meat, alternating with vegetables. If you don't have skewers, tooth-picks will hold a lot of green peas.

When a child must stay in bed, he will want new things to look at, such as:

1. A kaleidoscope, magnifying glass, or periscope.

2. A goldfish or turtle in a bowl.

3. A narcissus growing.

4. A clock.

5. Balloons and mobiles.

6. Oriental flowers that open in water.

7. A mirror.

8. Different pictures on the bulletin board, screen, or walls.

He will want new things to hold, such as:

1. A flashlight.

2. A long key chain with assorted trinkets or charms.

3. A bean bag.

4. A hand puppet (draw or paint a face on a man's solid-colored sock or on a mitten).

He will want new things to do, such as:

1. Stringing paper clips.

2. Stringing buttons or spools with a long thread and a big needle.

3. Drawing on carbon paper. (It's easier if you staple the three sheets together.)

4. Painting on a desk blotter with ink or poster paint.

5. Blowing soap bubbles (liquid detergent diluted with a little water, plus a straw and a paper cup).

6. Making collages (see Things To Do).

7. Playing with modeling clay or wallpaper cleaner.

8. Sticking toothpicks in a scouring pad.

9. Punching holes with a paper punch, or stapling paper together with a staple.

10. Sharpening pencils or crayons with a pencil sharpener or a crayon sharpener.

11. Making a puzzle by coloring or drawing on a shirt cardboard, then cutting it into five or six pieces.

12. Coloring on a new drawing pad.

13. Playing with a spring-type metal tape measure.

14. Starting a lending library with friends (assuming his illness is not infectious or contagious).

He will like his old things too, such as:

1. Books.

2. Records.

3. Crayons, paste, scissors, and colored chalk.

4. Favorite toys.

-- and --

He will want YOU.

When he wants you, he can ring a bell, blow a whistle, or call through a megaphone. And he will be tired of being alone, and he will want you to be tired of being without him, and he will want you to stay.

1. You can set up the board in his room and iron.

2. While you iron, you can talk, or tell stories, or play games.
   a. Game one: "I see something in this room and it's blue."
   b. Game two: "I hear something . . . what do I hear?"
   c. Game three: "What is a word that sounds like Billy?" (Milly, spilly, chilly, dilly, and silly.)

3. You can prepare dinner, or part of it, with his help: shelling peas, snipping off ends of beans (with blunt scissors), or cracking and shelling walnuts (you crack and he shells).

4. You can paste the photos in the family album and bring it up to date.

5. You can sew buttons on his shirts, glue his plastic soldiers, and tape all the torn books.

6. You can wash all the windows in his room and clean the wood-work.

7. He can dictate a letter to his grandmother or special friend. He is certain to mention somewhere in the letter that he is sick, and can be almost sure of a reply.

> Dear Grandmother,
>
> How are you?
>
> I am sick.
>
> Love,
>
> Billy.

VERY SPECIAL EVENTS

Christmas is coming,
The goose is growing fat.
Please to put a penny in an old man's hat.

—Nursery Rhyme

HOLIDAYS

Children don't know the reasons for some holidays, but they still enjoy any extra treats or adventures which the holiday brings with it.

The calendar shows many holidays, but for small children the feeling of the parents or the atmosphere of the neighborhood determines what happens.

From the standpoint of small children, the more holidays celebrated the better.

It's surprising that efforts put forth for the children are equally fun for the adults.

Halloween

Halloween means dressing up—dressing up to go out after dark to ring doorbells and have people put goodies in your sack. It is easy to dress two-year-olds for this occasion. Being uninhibited, they will ring doorbells wearing their everyday clothes and a lampshade on their head. Another disguise is father's old hat and a black mustache.

But when they get older, they want to be something or somebody. If you have a talent with the sewing machine, this is no problem for you. You can run up ballerina and clown costumes for all your children.

Warning: Don't spend too much effort because they often take a notion not to wear your creation.

Here are some costume suggestions for mothers who either have no patience with sewing or very little time or money:

Masks: Let the child decorate a paper bag with crayons or poster paint before you cut the eyes, nose, and mouth. He can paste yarn for hair, mustache, sideburns or beard, or tape pieces of soda straws for whiskers. If he doesn't want to wear his mask, add handles and he can use it for a "trick-or-treat" bag when he goes collecting.

Man from Mars: Cut off or roll up the bottom of a brown-paper bag for the headpiece. Cut an opening in the bag the size of his face. Scotch tape a piece of cellophane over the opening. On a white undershirt, use crayons to make a lightning streak. He can wear shorts or a swimming suit, long black socks or boots.

A Witch: An old black dress can be pinned up or a black blouse will cover most small children. He will need a fireplace broom or child's broom with black and orange crepe-paper streamers attached with a rubber band. The hat can be purchased or made by first making a cone shape from a sheet of black paper, 12" x 18". Add the brim with scotch tape or paste.

A Ghost: Put an old pillowcase over the child's head and cut openings in the side for his arms. Cut circles for eyes, nose, and mouth, and outline in black crayon. Tie a ribbon around the neck.

A Skeleton: Same as for ghost, except outline bones with black poster paint or black crayon.

A Pirate: Tie a red bandana around the child's head. He can wear real earrings or brass curtain rings attached by scotch tape. Tuck his trousers in rubber boots or cowboy boots, or notch a pair of old blue jeans. A rubber knife or cardbord knife held between the teeth is fierce.

A Queen: A crown can be made of cardboard covered with gold or silver paper. Scallop the top of the crown and add sequins or colored stars. An old lace tablecloth or curtain can be draped and pinned. Queens need lots of jewelry.

Nylon stocking over the face: Very spooky. A child will probably not wear it very long, but let him try it out on the family.

97

A Squaw: Tie a ribbon or piece of sheet around the child's head. Put a feather in the back. Wrap a blanket around her and pin it with a safety pin. Wrap a dolly in a small blanket and pin this on the back of the blanket. Wear bedroom slippers or moccasins.

A Brave: Wear the feather in the middle of the forehead. Decorate the body with war paint from a lipstick or red poster paint. Wear shorts and bedroom slippers. If it's a cold day, decorate only the face and cut off one of father's khaki shirts and fringe the bottom of it. Do the same with an old pair of the child's trousers. Hang a tom-tom made from an oatmeal carton around his neck so he will have his hands free. (See <u>You Can Make Your Own Music</u>).

Costumes from Sleepers—

Black Cat: Dye the sleepers and an old snow cap with black dye. To make the tail, sew a long strip of black material and stuff with newspaper, old nylon stockings, or cotton batting. Attach to back of sleepers. Ears can be made from heavy black paper or cardboard covered with black material and sewed to the cap. An eyebrow pencil, black crayon, or burned cork are all good for making the whiskers on the child's face.

Rabbit: The sleepers do not need to be dyed. Attach a piece of cotton on the back for the tail. The long ears can be cut from cardboard and covered with pink material and attached to a white snow suit cap. Make whiskers with eye brow pencil or ink.

Leopard: The tail and ears are the same as that of the black cat's. Cover sleepers and cap with black and brown circles, making them with either crayons or paint.

<u>Advice</u>—If you do not recognize what a child's costume represents, do not ask him what he is.

Jack-o-lanterns:

Most parents cut the top from the pumpkins, let the child scoop the seeds out, and that is his part in making the jack-o-lantern; the parents then proceed to make the face while the child watches.

Jack-o-lanterns don't need to have the conventional look, and they certainly won't if you let your child do the carving. Most kitchens have a paring knife sharp enough to cut pumpkins and dull enough not to cut fingers.

If your child is small or the pumpkins are hard to cut, let him draw the face with a pencil and you can follow the lines he has made.

Christmas

One suggestion for keeping Christmas civilized, eliminating a lot of bad tempers and Christmas nerves (which also accompany the holiday) is to plan with the calendar the four weeks preceding Christmas. You might make a calendar from around December 1 to December 25 on a large sheet of cardboard and hang it in a prominent place in the kitchen. Arrange the projects you hope to accomplish something like this:

Children can participate in the following projects—

First week:

Shelled walnuts:
> Crack and shell walnuts (or other nuts) and send each grandmother a jarful.

String boxes:
> Cover the top and bottom of a shoe box separately with paper that the child has decorated with one of these three methods as described in the section Things To Do - potato stamping, finger painting, or spatter painting on either brown wrapping paper or shelf paper. Put three balls of string or ribbon in the box and unwind a few inches of each ball. In the top of the box, poke three holes with an ice pick and pull the string through the top of the lid an inch or so. Good gift for grandfathers or aunts.

Candle holders:
> With a brace and a bit, bore holes the size of the candle in interesting pieces of driftwood. A candle board can be made by drilling holes in a piece of wood 2" deep, 4" wide, and 12" - 21" in length. Five-year-olds love to use a brace and bit.

Bookmark:
> With scissors, cut the corner of an envelope to make a triangle. Even your two-year-old can color it or paint it.

Decorated shopping bags:
> Paint or decorate with crayon five-cent shopping bags.

Knitting boxes:
> Already described under section called Things To Save (see "Oatmeal Boxes").

Book:
> Staple together several sheets of paper in book form. Let the child draw with pencil, crayon, or colored chalk, or cut pictures from magazines and paste in the book. Any comments he makes should be written in quotes.

Telephone pad or memo pad:
> Attach scratch pad to one of the child's finger paintings which has been pasted to a piece of cardboard. Tie a pencil on a long string and attach to cardboard.

Napkin holders:
> Children can paint ham-bone rings (which you have saved throughout the year) with bright enamel. Put a paper napkin through the ring so friends will know what they are for (see Things to Save and Why).

Planters:
> A piece of ivy, philodendron, or a bulb can be planted in a one-pound coffee can. Cover the outside of the can with some of your child's art work.

Burlap place mats:
> Burlap is easy for children to fringe, comes in gay colors, and makes useful gifts as place mats. After the child has unraveled one-half inch on all four sides, sew on the machine to prevent further unraveling.

Hot pad holder:
> Have the child decorate with crayons or paint the inside of one paper plate and the outside of another. The plate that has been colored on the outside is cut in half and stapled to the other plate to form the pocket. At the top of the plate, punch two holes and tie a bow with yarn.

Presents Mothers Can Make for Children.

This is what you do during nap time and after 8 p.m. Though it might be a good idea to start some of the projects during July, others will take very little time and all are inexpensive.

Sock horse:
> Stuff a man's sock with cotton batting. After you have stuffed from the toe to the heel, stick a broomstick or mop stick in the sock and continue stuffing around the stick until it is full. Stick three or four thumbtacks through the sock to hold to the stick. Sew two buttons on for eyes. Sew two fingers cut from an old glove and they will look like ears. A piece of rawhide thong (from the shoe-repair shop) can be tied to look like a harness and can be used for the reins. You can make it fancy by adding a yarn mane. If you like girl horses, add eyelashes (felt or yarn).

Bean bags:
> Any scrap of material can be cut into any shape and partially filled with navy beans. The material can be decorated or plain.

Money bags:
> Sew three sides of the pouch together, leaving the top open.

Hem the top and run a shoe lace through it. Fill with money and tie shoelace.

Shoe bags:

For toys or shoes. Sew six or nine pockets on a piece of sturdy material such as heavy denim or canvas. These are fun to decorate with textile paint.

Glove dolls:

Cut off all the fingers and thumb of an old glove. Stuff all five with cotton. Using the thumb for the body and the head of the doll, tie a string to form the head. The fingers form the arms and legs. Sew parts together and dress with scraps of material.

Clothes-pin dolls:

Paint a face on the top of the clothes pin. Stick the "legs" in modeling clay to hold. Decorate with scraps of material.

Surprise balls:

Cut crepe paper that comes in folds in one-inch strips. Unfold the strips and start winding in the shape of a ball. Have several small trinkets wrapped in tissue paper ready to be hidden inside the ball as you wrap the crepe paper. These could be a balloon, a dime, a ring, a chain, perhaps with small charms to attach to it. Candies and a poem or some message to the child would complete the ball. Secure ball with sticky tape. The child will like the streamers as well as the gifts inside.

Jingle-bell bracelets:

Sew three or four bells to a strip of eleastic or a half-inch width of ribbon long enough to tie around the wrist or ankle (see You Can Make Your Own Music).

A Billy Book

A "Billy Book" is about a little boy named Billy. It can also be about a girl named Jane, or for whomever you want to make a book. A book for a child about himself is very satisfying to his ego.

Several weeks before Christmas, ask the mothers of the children you plan to make the books for to give you some snapshots of their children. Assure them they will get the pictures back, and they will be curious and excited.

The story will vary with each child, but here is an example of one book, done for three children in the same family.

Page One

Once upon a time there was a boy named William, only his best friends all called him Billy. Everyone knows that Billy is a good name, because it rhymes with:

SILLY

WILLY NILLY

and

FILLY (a young horse)

(Photograph of the Hero at his Birthday Party)

Page Two

Once upon a time there was also a boy named Mark, and Mark is what his best friends called him. Everyone knows that Mark is an excellent name, because it rhymes with:

PARK (where you play)

HARK, HARK, THE LARK

and

BARK (like a dog)

(Photograph of the other Hero, on his trike)

Page Three

There was also a little tiny girl whose name was Katherine, which is an especially good name because it doesn't rhyme with anything.

(Photograph of the Heroine in diapers)

Page Four

Billy and Mark and Katherine all had the same last name, because they belonged to the same family. For the same reason, they lived in the same house. It was a new house, too.

You can draw a picture of their house, and underneath the picture you say:

44 Hillcrest Drive

Central Point

Oregon

United States

North America

Western Hemisphere

World

Universe

Page Five

Billy and Mark and Katherine did all kinds of things every day, only Billy and Mark did them longer, because they were older. They could do lots of tricks, and hop on one foot (not clear across the living room, though), and they could swim, and sing some songs, and Billy could even write his own name on the blackboard.

(Draw picture of boy, writing his name)

Page Six

Katherine could not hop on one foot at all!
But she could hop on two feet!

(Draw picture of girl hopping)

Page Seven

And then, one day—along came Christmas!

(Draw picture of Christmas tree)

Page Eight

Two very old friends of Billy's and Mark's and Katherine's, who used to be neighbors, wanted to wish them a Very Merry Christmas. The old friends were Chris and Peter Botsford, who lived at 111 E. Floresta Drive, Menlo Park, California, United States, North America, Western Hemisphere, World, Universe.

(Photograph of Chris and Peter, children of the author of the "Billy Book")

Page Nine

So they made up this song:

> Merry Christmas to you,
> From Peter and Chris,
> In our neighborhood,
> It is you that we miss.
>
> Merry Christmas to you,
> From Chris and Pete,
> We hope that we all
> Will soon again meet!

Second week: The second week of December could be called the Fruit-Cake Week or Popcorn-Ball Week or Cookie Week. Cookies are the most fun for children, and some they make can be put in boxes to be sent out of town. Either make a great many different kinds, or concentrate on your specialty. The plain sugar cookie to be cut out with Christmas cutters is easy for children and fun to decorate.

If you want the cookies to hang on the tree, make a hole with an ice pick near the top before you bake them.

Cinnamon drops, gum drops, and raisins can be stuck on the cookie before it is baked.

Children love to use icing tubes and can manage them successfully in decorating the cookie after it is baked. If you want to make colored sugar, put two or three drops of food coloring into a jar with a tight lid, add the sugar and shake.

Popcorn balls are easy to make. The syrup can be colored red or green, or they can be wrapped in colored cellophane. They are pretty tied on packages, hung on the tree, or on the front-door wreath.

Stuffing dates with nuts and rolling in powdered sugar is an old stand-by Christmas goodie that even two-year-olds can manage.

Third week: The third week is called "Decorating-the-House Week." The children can make some of these decorations with little or no assistance from you. Homemade decorations for the tree and the house are a big part of understanding the spirit of Christmas, also of getting everyone into the spirit. Most of these decorations can be saved from year to year.

Chains—A five-inch strip of colored paper cut one-half inch wide and pasted together to form a circle is the first part of the chain. The second strip slips through the circle and the two ends are pasted together to make another circle, ad infinitum.

Oriental lanterns—These are described in the section Things To Make. Several lanterns can be strung on a string.

Spirals—Another paper craft that is fun and easy for small children and the effect is good. First cut a circle of colored paper or heavy foil. Draw with a pencil a line which follows around and around the circle, ending in the center of the circle. After the child has done a few, he will be able to cut without the aid of the line. Paste two spirals together to get one very long one. (See Making Things.)

104

Covered walnuts—Wrap aluminum foil around a walnut, pressing the foil smooth but extending the paper on one side of the nut so a ribbon can be tied around it. Tie a loop in the ribbon so it can be hung over a branch of the tree.

Snowflakes—Fold a square of paper in half and then in half again. Let the child cut and notch and scallop. Always interesting in design and proof that no two snowflakes are ever alike. To be pasted or scotch taped on windows.

Santa Apples—Start with a shiny red apple. Using six toothpicks, put one near the stem for the head, two for the arms, two for the legs, and one to support him. Stick marshmallows on the toothpicks for the head, arms, and legs. Put raisins on the end of the toothpicks for hands and feet. Poke whole cloves down the front of the apple for buttons, and whole cloves for eyes, nose, and mouth. Tuck a piece of cotton under his chin. Flatten out a prune and put it on his head for a cap.

Christmas trees—A. Spread an ice-cream cone with powdered sugar frosting which has been tinted green. Before the frosting dries, press popped corn all over the tree. Cinammon drops and cut-up gum drops stuck around the popcorn make the tree look as if it has lights. Make several and have a forest. Arrange on tables. B. A larger tree could be made from cardboard. Fold a sheet 12'' x 18'' into a cone shape. Trim and staple. Decorate.

Pipe cleaners or Twist-'Ems—Twist these into any shape that pleases you—a wreath, a tree, a bell.

Cornucopias—Fold a half circle of construction paper so the outside edges overlap enough to hold together with staples or paste. Punch a hole in the opposite side from the pasted side, and use a ribbon to hang it from the tree. Fill with candy, if you like.

More snowflakes—Tie fifteen or twenty soda straws together by drawing a string as tight as you can get it around the middle of all the straws. As you draw the string tight, the straws will spread. Hang on the tree, or hang from the ceiling with different lengths of thread. Cellophane straws are particularly attractive as they catch the light and sparkle.

Strung cranberries—Cranberries and popcorn strung alternately look pretty, but popcorn is a little tedious for small children. Use a large needle, double thread, and tie strings together for a continuous chain.

Decorated pine cones—A. Children love to paint them with poster paints or spray them gold, silver, white or pink, using the new pressurized paint cans. It is rather expensive. B. Popcorn and cranberries are easily stuck in the pinecones and look very effective. C. Touch the tips of the cone with glue and sprinkle glitter over it while the glue still is wet. D. Put glue on the tips of the cone and press tiny glass balls (which come in strings like beads) on the ends.

Milk-bottle tops—Let the child put paste on both sides of the top, and then sprinkle with Christmas "snow" while the paste is still wet. Punch hole and hang on tree, adding ribbon.

Newspaper ornaments—(For mothers to make) Wad a piece of dry newspaper until it is round. Cover the wad with strips of paper (4" x 1") which have been dipped in a thin solution of wheat-paste flour and water. Wipe off excessive paste and set aside until dry. Note: this often takes two or three days. Paint with poster paint and decorate. An apple, orange, or gourd can be covered with the strips of pasted paper as described above and cut in half, when dry, with a sharp knife. When cutting, be careful not to cut the fruit, just to it. After a string has been taped to the inside, put the two halves together again and wrap the hollow ball with more pasted strips. Decorate.

Bells can be made from paper cups. Stuff a wad of wet paper at the top and cover the inside and outside of the paper cup with the pasted strips. Allow to dry, paint and decorate.

A Christmas candle—A very good idea for all those who want to know "how many more days." From the top of a long candle paste the number 12, 11, 10, 9, 8, and on down to number 1, and then a message of "Merry Christmas." Each day, starting with the twelfth day before Christmas, the candle is burned one number.

See sections Things To Do and Making Things for more Christmas ideas, such as painting balloons, wire sculpture, etc.

Children's Trees

If the children want a tree of their own to put their own decorations on:

1. Buy two trees, maybe one could be a live tree.

2. Try one of the following:

   A. Cut branches off the family tree and stick in a bucket of wet sand.

B. Find attractive branches of oak, pine, or pyracantha and set in a can of plaster of Paris or wet sand. Children can spray them with a snow bomb or paint the branches with white poster paint. They will also like mixing up a thick solution of soap-flakes and water and rubbing "snow" on the branches.

"Food" trees have a special appeal to small children.

Lollipop tree: Hang lollipops all over the tree. When their friends come to call, they are to cut lollipops from the branch and give them to their friends.

Cookie tree: Before the cookie goes in the oven, make a hole in the dough so a ribbon can be run through the cookie. Hang from the tree same as lollipops, and they are to be shared in the same way.

Candy-cane tree: As above.

Popcorn-ball tree: Wrap popcorn balls in colored cellophane and hang from tree.

Treasure-chest tree: This decoration is made from the chocolate candy that comes wrapped in gold paper and looks like gold money. Heat the end of an ice pick, make a hole through each coin and hang on the tree with ribbon.

Gum-drop tree: Stick gum drops on a small branch; one that has been painted white is more effective.

Other suggestions for decorating Christmas trees and branches are:

All balloons: All one color or many colors is equally pretty. Stick colored stars on the balloons, or decorate with poster paints.

All pine cones: Whether or not the pine cones are painted is a matter of taste. A tree with small unpainted pine cones, all hanging from red ribbons, is very effective.

All pipe cleaners: Use colored pipe cleaners. On a small branch, twist them into the shapes of animals, people, Christmas bells, wreaths, or trees. Twist red-and-white pipe cleaners together to look like a candy cane.

A tree for the birds: If you have an evergreen growing outside, hang cranberry and popcorn strings or squares of dried bread on it. Birds don't seem to mind, however, if their Christmas treats are hung from a potted lemon or flowering plum.

Fourth week: The fourth week finds you ready and relaxed, waiting for Santa if you are like some of us, or frantically doing all of the things you didn't have time for in the first, second, and third week, if you are like Most of us.

Easter

Before the Easter bunny comes to your house, tell him not to leave expensive presents for your child, like stuffed animals or tricycles; for if he does, he is then a villain to the child next door who was left a chocolate-covered egg.

Easter bunnies are very co-operative. 1 They will fill grass nests which you have made and hidden around the house. 2 They will hide jelly beans along the baseboards. 3 They will bring only hard-cooked eggs to a sugar-free household. Or 4 they will bring their own variety of nests, baskets, and eggs.

Easter baskets can be made from cottage-cheese cartons which have been wrapped with strips of pastel crepe paper and stapled or pasted to the side of the carton. Wrap a cardboard handle and staple to the sides. Ice-cream cartons, strawberry baskets, and oatmeal cartons split in half also make good Easter Baskets. (See Things To Save And Why.)

Easter eggs can be dyed green with spinach juice, brown with coffee, yellow with onion skins, and red with beet juice. A single plant, such as a pansy, planted in half an eggshell, makes a nice gift for a small child to give for Easter.

Easter-egg tree: Set a small, attractive branch into a cottage-cheese container and pour plaster of Paris around the branch. When the plaster of Paris is hard, tear away the container. Paint or spray the branch.

Blown eggs: With a pin, poke a hole in the top and bottom of a raw egg. Blow over a large bowl (children love to blow eggs). If the egg is stubborn, puncture the yolk with a pin. After the insides have been blown out, decorate the shell with Easter-egg dyes and hang from the branch. Use the eggs for scrambling. Use the branch for Christmas decorations also.

CHILDREN'S BIRTHDAYS AND PARTIES

"At last," the Dodo said, "everyone has won, and all must have prizes."

—Alice in Wonderland,
Lewis Carroll

CHILDREN'S BIRTHDAYS and PARTIES

If you have no birthday traditions, you might start a few.

1. Other members of the family can decorate a birthday chair with crepe paper and make a crown for the honored one.

2. Every member of the family can make something for the child— a scrapbook, a poem, a picture.

3. Put a gift in the same place each year—under his pillow, under his bed, under his plate.

4. Learn a new birthday song:
Oh! Jimmy, dear, we'll sing-a-ling-a-ling
This little song for you.
We hope there'll be some thing-a-ling-a-ling
That we can do for you.
In autumn, winter, spring-a-ling-a-ling
And all the whole year through.
We'll sing-a-ling-a-ling
And ting-a-ling-a-ling
And sing-a-ling-a-ling for you.

(On the "ling-a-lings," you hit your water glass gently with a spoon.)

5. The child whose birthday is being celebrated gives small gifts to his brothers and sisters.

6. If your child doesn't like cake but is crazy for pancakes, put his candles on a stack of pancakes and sing to him at breakfast. Or he may be a fancier of a certain kind of pie and would be happy and surprised with five candles on top of a lemon meringue.

Presents that children like do not always come from toy stores.

1. A flashlight.
2. A zippered duffel bag.
3. Canteens, pup tents, and other items from surplus stores.
4. A decoy duck (from sporting goods store).
5. A 25' length of hose.
6. A hammer, saw, and a bag of nails.

7. Scratch pads, colored pencils or crayons, carbon paper and paper clips.
8. A box of Band Aids and a roll of sticky tape.
9. A stapler and a punch.
10. A box of paper cups and several packages of Kool-Aid.
11. Money.
12. A turtle, fish, or parakeet.

Here are some suggestions for parties for different ages.

First year: When the baby is one year old, it is usually better for everyone if the birthday celebration is forgotten. If you feel something should be made of the occasion, some suggestions are:

1. Make a cake and put a candle on it. Mother can invite all her friends and all their babies to join the festivity. Mothers can eat cake and drink coffee, while the babies totter and fall, nurse or drink milk from bottles, and mess in the cake.

2. Make a cake and put a candle on it. Mother and Father can sing Happy Birthday to baby, blow out the candle, tuck baby in bed, and then eat the cake.

3. Leave the baby with a sitter or with grandmother and celebrate the occasion by going out to dinner.

Second year: If the child is in a neighborhood with a lot of other children, you can invite all the children in the neighborhood, or let older brother and sister invite their friends for cupcakes and ice-cream bars at three o'clock. No one is to bring the child a gift, and after the cake and ice cream have been consumed hand out balloons, and the party is over.

Third year: This is your last chance to have the birthday as you want it. You can still invite your friends and their children and include a special playmate or two from the neighborhood. The child will begin to enjoy some of the tradition of ice cream and cake and new clothes and new toys. Three-year-olds like circle and musical games suggested for them in the following chapter. Records, movies, plasticene, soap bubbles, and balloons will keep them busy and happy.

Fourth and Fifth year: There will be big talk and big plans for these birthdays. Not all children want parties. Some want to celebrate by going down town to Daddy's office and typing on his typewriter. Others want a ride on a train or a trip to the zoo, a ferryboat ride, or a picnic in the park. The privilege of staying all night with a favorite relative or friend is what some request, while others beg to eat out at a local restaurant.

Parties will have taken on a prestige value. "You can't come to my Happy Birthday!" is a common threat.

There is a lot to be said for the idea of having the same number of guests as the child is old; i.e. four years old, four guests. This is a fine idea except when you live in a sociable neighborhood and would have to leave someone out.

The four-or five-year-old who is giving the party can plan with Mother the guest list, the invitations, the menu, and shop for favors to give him the sense of pleasure from giving as well as getting gifts.

More and more the traditional cake and ice-cream party from three to five in the afternoon is being replaced by morning parties including lunch, or four to six parties including supper. The obvious reasons for this are: mid-morning or mid-afternoon partying spoils meals and upsets nap routines.

State on the invitation that you will bring the children home from the party. This eliminates hovering parents who come too early, or worse, those who come too late.

Even though a party is a product of civilization, it doesn't always work out that way when the participants aren't fully civilized yet.

Things That Often Happen at Birthday Parties

1. The host cannot bear it when Happy Birthday is sung to him. It is too overpowering an experience, so he hides under the table, puts his fingers in his ears, or makes loud noises.

2. You send your child to a party next door, and in five minutes he wanders home again.

3. The host greets his guests by saying, "Where's the present?"

4. The host won't let anyone touch his presents.

5. The host goes in his room and won't come out.

6. Your child refuses to relinquish the present. He thinks it was for him. It may help some to explain beforehand, "This is for Sally, because it is her birthday. Sally will give you ice cream and cake."

7. Mothers try too hard to make the child perform conventionally. They often plan Pin the Tail on the Donkey and find that no one will wear the blindfold.

Party Food

Finger foods are what children like best and eat best.

This would include sandwiches, such as cream cheese and olive, tuna, peanut butter and jelly, buttered raisin bread, and egg salad.

It's a good idea to make several kinds and to cut the whole sandwiches into fourths.

Carrot sticks, celery sticks, pieces of cauliflower, and green-pepper rings offer a variety in vegetables.

Pitted ripe olives are a favorite with most children, and if you want to make yourself popular, give each child ten, to stick on the ends of each finger. If you don't feel so generous, put a carrot stick through two or three.

Potato chips, corn chips, cheese puffs, etc.

Jello with fruit added can be molded in paper muffin cups and served with plastic throw-away spoons.

A five-cent bag of salted peanuts, a box of raisins, or a package of animal cookies can be eaten at the party or taken home (children like to take things home).

If you are going to serve the birthday cake at the party, cut very small pieces with assurances that they can have more.

Cupcakes served with a lighted candle are often more fun for the guests.

Ice-cream cups are the easiest to have at a party, but maybe your child has his heart set on orange popsicles. Popsicles, cones, and bars are all very drippy and better for outside eating.

Orange juice or apple juice could replace milk at the party luncheon or supper. Half root beer and half milk is another good party drink. Or chocolate milk with a dipper of ice cream. Cut paper straws in half if you are using paper cups.

Two Successful Parties for Preschoolers

The Barbecue. A cook-your-own-hot-dog party for warm-weather birthdays.

Invitations could be written on brown wrapping paper.

Food: Hot dogs, buns, potato salad, relishes, cokes in bottles, and ice cream sandwiches or marshmallows.

Favors: If mothers have time and like to sew, they can make aprons for the girls and chef's aprons for the boys.
Red neckerchiefs and neckerchief slides would suit both sexes.
Crepe-paper lariats from the dime store are fun and suitable for the occasion.

The Circus Party.

Invitations: Blow up balloons and write time and place, etc., with colored poster paints. The host can deliver the balloons in the neighborhood. State on invitation "Bring your bike, trike, or wagon or wild animals." (A goldfish, turtle, dog, cat, and little sister qualify as wild animals.)

Dressing up: Some children dress up only for Halloween, and some children play-act a different character every day with costume; most children are glad to get a chance to do it more often. Boys who don't want to wear their spook costumes to this party can come as cowboys, Indians, or pirates. Tarzan is easy and a good costume for summertime. The tattooed man can wear shorts and poster-paint decorations.

Girls can wear dress-up clothes from mother's closet, or be a queen, an angel, a witch or a squaw with few materials and lots of imagination. Dancing girls can wear their best Sunday-School dress and patent leather shoes. A fat lady stuffs a pillow under big sister's dress and draws the belt tight.

Other costume ideas are listed in the Holiday section under "Halloween."

Activities and Games:
Cut one-inch strips of colored crepe paper and let the children decorate their trikes or wagons and have a parade down the block or around the patio.

Make a peanut lei for each child by stringing shelled peanuts on a heavy thread. (Children can help with this.)

Fishing for surprises—To make the pole, attach string to any sturdy stick, and on the end of the string fasten a small paper bag with a safety pin. A sheet hung over backs of chairs, or a clothesline, conceals the "fish." Gifts such as bubble gum, rabbit's feet, bean shooters, whistles, magnets, make the fishermen happy.

Pin the Nose on BoBo—The same as pin the tail on the donkey, except you draw a clown face on a sheet of cardboard and use red-circle noses to see who gets the closest. (Most children who have reached four don't mind being blindfolded.)

Clown hats—This could be the favor if it is a birthday party. Form a cone from a sheet of paper 12" x 18". Trim and staple together. Decorate the hat by pasting circles or long strips of paper, or paint, or crayon designs. Use a crepe-paper tassle at the top and attach ribbons on each side so it can tie under the chin.

Food:
Sandwiches, relishes, pink lemonade, popcorn in white paper bags.

Ice-cream clown—turn an ice-cream cone upside down on a dipper of ice cream which is on a paper plate. In the ice cream, make a face with red hots, gum drops, or raisins.

Circus cakes—Use animal crackers or plastic animals from the dime store around the edges of a frosted cake. Use graham-cracker crumbs on the top and around the bottom of the cake for sawdust effect.

or

Merry-go-round Cake—Use eight or ten colored candy sticks around the edge of the cake. On top of the sticks is an inverted paper plate, the top of which has been frosted like the cake. Use animal crackers or plastic animals at each candy-stick pole to resemble merry-go-round animals.

It's nice, occasionally, to have a party that isn't a birthday.

The following party suggestions can justifiably be called "informals."

The Hose Party: All the children are invited to come over and run through the hose or sprinkler. Tell them to wear their swimming suits and bring a towel and pair of shorts. Water pistols would make a good favor. Probably the only time everyone had a water pistol at the same time.

The Watermelon-Hose Party: Same as the Hose Party except first you eat watermelon, run through the sprinkler, turn the water off, change into dry clothes, and have surprises for each child hidden in the sandbox. Surprises could be magnets, soap bubbles, or a four-piece balsa-wood glider.

The Paper-bag Party: Pack everyone's lunch in a paper bag and help the children decide where a good place to eat (outside) would be. This could also be called "camping" if you provide a few blankets and a thermos of something.

A Cookie-making Party (for a small crowd): It's not really a cookie-making party, it's a cookie-decorating party, because the dough is all made. But they get to roll it out and use the cutters and squirt tubes, and they get to spread icing on them when they are baked and then decorate them with colored sugar, raisins, gum drops, and cinammon drops. And they get to keep the cookies they made, to take home and eat. Whether a cookie-making party is a success or not depends on several things. A big enough table to work on, enough materials to work with, and a mother. Valentine's Day, Easter, and Christmas are good times to make cookies, but a Santa Claus in the middle of July tastes good to little children, too.

114

GAMES

"I put my right foot in,
I take my right foot out,
I give my foot a shake, shake, shake,
And turn myself about."

GAMES

The following games are suitable to preschool-aged children, if they are allowed to play them in their own way.

Small children never get tired of the repetition of London Bridge. When the bridge falls down on the fair lady, she continues to go under and doesn't follow the more complicated method of joining behind one one of the bridges. In Musical Chairs, when the music stops and the child is left without a chair, he stays in the game and the game proceeds without removing the child or another chair.

In guessing games, children "tell," in hiding games, they peek. But it is fun for them and you will only bewilder them by trying to impose stricter rules or organization into their games.

If the occasion is a party and you want to give prizes, pass a plate of bubble gum or balloons to the winner, those who participated, and those who watched. Giving a prize to the winner only, creates bad feeling with all the losers.

Circle Games

Cobbler Cobbler: One child stands in the center of the circle with his eyes covered. The other children pass a shoe behind their backs and chant:

Cobbler, Cobbler, mend my shoe,
Have it done by half past two,
Stitch it up, and stitch it down,
Now see where my shoe is found.

The person in the center guesses who is holding the shoe behind him and then that person is "it."

Variation: The children can pass a marble from hand to hand, while the one who is "it" has left the room. All the children sit with their hands clenched and "it" guesses who has the marble.

Drop the Handkerchief: Children form a circle. One child runs (or walks) around the outside of the circle and drops the handkerchief behind one of the other children. That child picks up the handkerchief and tries to tag the first child before he gets back to his place.

<u>Woof-Woof</u>: While the child who is "it" is in the next room, the others decide who will be the "woof-woof." When "it" returns, the children are sitting in a circle with their hands covering their faces. The child selected then says, "Woof-woof" trying to disguise his voice and his position. When "it" guesses who the "woof-woof" is, the "woof-woof" becomes "it."

Musical Games

<u>Farmer in the Dell</u>: The children form a circle and one child is selected to be the farmer. He stands in the center of the circle while the song is sung.

> The farmer in the dell
> The farmer in the dell
> Heigho! the derry oh,
> The farmer in the dell.
>
> The farmer picks a wife
> The farmer picks a wife
> Heigho! the derry oh!
> The farmer picks a wife.

At the end of this verse, the child in the center chooses one of the children to be his wife and she joins him in the middle of the circle. The verse is sung again, and at the conclusion, the wife chooses a child, and the child chooses a nurse, and the nurse a dog, and the dog a cat, and the cat a mouse, and the mouse a cheese, and the cheese stands alone.

<u>London Bridge</u>: Two children form a bridge by holding their hands together above their heads. The other children walk under the bridge singing this verse:

> London Bridge is falling down,
> Falling down, falling down,
> London Bridge is falling down,
> My fair lady.

The bridge collapses on the one child on the final line, "My fair lady."

<u>Ring-Around-a-Rosey</u>: Children form a circle, join hands, and sing:

> Ring-Around-a-Rosey
> Pocket full of posey
> Ashes, Ashes, all fall down.

They all fall down on the last line.

<u>Merry-Go-Round</u>: The children gallop around in a circle singing this rhyme:

The merry-go-round went round and round,
And the children laughed and laughed.
So many were going round and round,
That the merry-go-round collapsed.

At the word "collapsed," everyone sits on the floor.

Musical Chairs: Put two rows of chairs together, back to back. The children walk around the chairs while the music is playing and when the music stops, all hurry to get in a chair, because there is one less chair than child.

Musical Bean Bag: The children stand in a circle and pass a bean bag from hand to hand around the circle. When the music stops, the child left holding the bean bag either steps inside the circle, outside the circle, or continues to play.

Looby Loo: This action game is very popular with small children. It is not necessary to have the record. Children join hands and walk around the circle singing:

Here we go Looby Loo
Here we go Looby Lie
Here we go Looby Loo
All on a Saturday Night.

Children drop hands and sing:

I put my right foot in
I take my right foot out
I give my foot a shake, shake, shake
And turn myself about.

Chorus again of "Here we go Looby Loo," followed by same action as above, using:
left foot in and out—right hand in and out
left hand in and out—little head in and out
whole self in and out.

Hokey Pokey: A musical game very similar to Looby Loo, but not as effective without the record.

You put your right foot in,
You take your right foot out,
You put your right foot in, and you
    shake it all about.
You do the Hokey Pokey and you turn yourself around.
That's what it's all about.
(clap this last line out).

This first verse is performed with all the children standing in a circle. You "Hokey Pokey" by raising your hands above your head and shaking them as you turn a full circle.

117

Repeat the above verse and action using:

> left foot in and out
> right hand in and out
> left hand in and out
> right elbow in and out
> left elbow in and out
> right hip in and out
> left hip in and out
> whole self in and out
> backside in and out

The game ends by doing the Hokey Pokey twice (this time raising arms from above the head to the floor), continuing to Hokey Pokey down on your knees, and slapping the floor on the final line, "That's what it's all about."

Hide and Seek

One child hides his eyes and counts. The others hide themselves. When all are hidden, he tries to find them.

Run and Chase Games

Join the Gang: One child is the leader. He stands on one side of the room, the other children on the other side. When he yells, "Join my gang!" they all run toward him and he tries to catch one of them. When he catches one, that child joins the leader and the two of them go back to their place and yell, "Join my gang!"

Black Cats and Pumpkins: The children are divided into two groups, standing on opposite sides of the room. The pumpkins turn their backs to the black cats and the black cats tiptoe very near to them and then yell, "Pumpkins, watch out!" The pumpkins turn around and try to catch the black cats. The black cats that are caught can either join the pumpkin team or go back to their own team. Next, the black cats catch the pumpkins. This game can be changed with the seasons. It can be Santa Claus and the Reindeers, or Easter Bunnies and Easter Eggs.

Traffic Lights: One child is the policeman. He stands on a chair and holds up a piece of green paper. All the children run until he holds up the red paper which he has in his other hand. He alternates red and green (or stop and go) until it is time to change policeman.

Tag: One child is "it." He chases the other children until he touches one. Then that child is "it." The only child he cannot "tag" is the one who just tagged him...expressed as "no-touch-back."

118

Guessing Games

Hiding the Peanut: One child leaves the room, and the other children decide where to hide the peanut. When he re-enters the room, the children tell him whether he is hot or cold until he finds it.

Who Am I?: In this game, Mother is "it." The children sit on chairs in a circle. The mother stands behind the circle with her eyes closed and feels head, face, and arms of the child. She asks questions such as, "Oh, oh, pigtails—is it a girl? (Children answer, some say "no.") "Does she have a little brother?" "Is her brother's name Douglas?" "Is she ticklish?" (tickle under chin) "Does she have red hair?" "Is it Elaine?" (Answer is "Yes.") Proceed to next child without looking.

Who Is It?: One child leaves the room. A child is selected from the group to be "it." The child returns to the room and tries to find out who "it" is by asking only "yes" and "no" questions, such as "Is 'it' a girl?" "Does 'it' have red keds on?" When she guesses who "it" is, "it," is the next to leave the room. (This game for five-year-olds only.)

The trouble with "it" games is, everyone wants to be "it."

Games of Skill

Beans in a Jar: Each child is given ten navy beans which he attempts to throw into a waste basket or cardboard carton from a chalk line on the floor.

Blowing the Feather: The child throws a light feather into the air and tries to keep it in the air by blowing (no hands). When the feather hits the ground, he passes the feather to the next child.

Soda-cracker Race: Give each child one double soda cracker. The one who can eat his the fastest and sing "Mary had a little lamb," is the winner.

Other Games

Sticky Balloons: Rub the balloon against your clothing a few seconds with brisk, fast motions. The balloon will stick to the wall or ceiling.

Fish: Tie a string on a stick. On the end of the string fasten a small paper bag with a safety pin. The child throws the "pole" over a sheet and you fill the paper bag with a gift. Pull on the string a couple of times so he will know when he has caught the fish.

119

Follow the Leader: One child is the leader and the rest line up behind him and mimic his actions. He may walk with his hands on his knees, fly like a bird, run, or just walk.

Follow the Trail: From a certain point, tie and start unwinding a ball of string. It can go indoors and out, upstairs and down, and at the end of the trail is a treasure for all. The treasure could be a shoe box full of small wrapped gifts.

Ball Games

For all of these games, a soft rubber ball about six to eight inches in diameter is most suitable.

Rolling the Ball: The children sit in a circle with their legs spread and their feet touching the next child. The child who starts rolling the ball calls out the name of the child for whom it is intended.

Bouncing the Ball: The children stand in two lines, one line facing the other. The child who starts the game throws the ball so that it bounces in the center of the two lines of the group only once, and calls out the name of the child who should catch it.

Balls in a Basket: Children stand a certain distance from a large wastepaper basket and throw the ball into the basket. (For indoors, rolled up socks are good "balls" for this game.)

Basketball: Remove the bottom from a bushel basket. Tie it to a post or tree, slightly above the child's head.

Tetherball: A three-inch pipe about eight feet long is set in the ground. A strong rope is tied near the top of the pipe and a tether ball is hung from the end. The ball should hang at waist level. The object of the game is to see which of the two players can wind the ball around the pole, with each hitting in opposite directions. Tetherball is one of the child's first experiences in competitive sports, and when he is in the second grade, you will learn a lot of rules concerning the game, but for preschoolers it is fun simply to bat the ball around the pole, whether they are alone or playing with several others.

Croquet: Another game small children can enjoy without rules. They like to hit the ball with the mallet. Wickets, of course, can be made from wire coat hangers.

Golf: Cut a broom handle to a suitable length for your child. Drill a hole at an angle in a block of wood 2" x 2" x 4", and insert handle. Sink jars, such as peanut-butter jars, in the ground at appropriate distances for the course.

TRAVELING WITH LITTLE CHILDREN

East, West, Home is Best

—Old Saw

TRAVELING WITH LITTLE CHILDREN

You can no longer impetuously decide to climb in your car and, ignoring all reservations, speed off to you know not where. Now you have to plan—and not be too disappointed if a case of measles at the last moment upsets your plans.

Here are some general, useful tips that will help to make traveling with little children more fun for everybody.

Tell them about the trip first.

This may sound elementary, but it's important. Children under six are apt to be quite stuffy and prefer their everyday existence to an extended trip. But if they know what to expect they won't feel too uprooted, and will enjoy their experience more. If you don't consider this necessary, imagine yourself dropped down into a foreign country, where everything is strange and you don't speak the language or understand the mores of the natives. If the house where you will visit has stairs, talk about stairs. And if Aunt Mildred is in a wheel chair, talk about that a little bit.

How to fix up your car for children:

One mother we talked to, who has done a great deal of traveling with her children while her husband was overseas, gave us this solution:

"A must is to fix the back-seat level for play and nap area. The best way to do this is to put in the two suitcases that have to come out when you stop at a motel, cover them with blankets, and drape an old bedspread (not scratchy) or sheet over that. I mention suitcases needed at night because, though you might think it difficult to undo the arrangement, it will need remaking by that time anyway, and this saves opening the trunk of the car.

I am a great believer in car seats, even for children as old as five. Children can see out better, it keeps them from bumping into one another, and fighting, and, of course, it is much safer, and therefore easier on the driver.

Try making a rule—only one child down at a time from his car seat to nap or play in the level area. Early in the morning, or after eating, when they are in a good frame of mind, they can both be down as a treat.

If they both want to lie down for naps at the same time, take out one car seat and pile it on top of the other. The smaller child can lie down on the seat, and the longer child on the built-up space.''

Pillows are comforting things to take. And an outdoor chaise mattress is a good kind of mattress for the back seat of a station wagon. Also, a bag for dirty laundry. And a denim bag, with draw strings, which is easy to make, can be tacked to the side of the car to hold small toys. Also a bag, or tin can, for waste paper and gum wrappers (paper bags break).

If you have a cigarette lighter in the back seat, remove it and cover the empty hole with strong tape. (Do this when they are not around, so you won't call their attention to it.)

Back-seat door handles can be removed on the inside by yourself or a mechanic.

Things to think about taking:

1. Container filled with snacks such as cheese or raisins.

2. Water, if the water supply en route is doubtful.

3. One way to solve the thirst problem is frozen juice. Wrap the can in a cloth so their hands won't freeze. Punch a hole and let them suck on it. They will usually have finished it before the juice melts.

4. If you may stop at rest rooms that may not be clean, take your own toilet-seat covers.

5. Washcloth and soap. This is also handy to keep them out of public rest rooms. They can wash their faces and hands at outdoor faucets or hoses.

6. Disposable diapers, if you are in that stage.

7. For carsickness: Ask your doctor for pills. Also take empty ice-cream cartons, sponges, tissues, a lemon or peppermints to suck.

8. First-aid kit.

9. Their own suitcase, which they may help pack.

10. Stroller, even for a three-year old, if you will do much walking (as at Zoo).

11. Song Book, if your repertoire is limited.

12. A friend for your child, especially if he is an only child.

Good toys for trips:

1. Their own, favorite cuddly doll or animal.

2. New and old books. (Old books, because they know the story by the pictures.)

3. Children's steering wheels, like the real steering wheel, so they can drive, too.

4. Adhesive or scotch tape to stick on back windows, or all over themselves.

5. Good goal: Ten-cent stores every so many miles to fill up bag with cheap toys. Cars and trucks to run around in among blankets are especially good.

6. Many children prefer articles bought at the hardware, stationery or jewelry counter to toys. Tiny sewing kits, with the needles removed, cheap and flashy rings, punchers tape, key rings—or even a collection of old bottle caps. An old purse, like mother's purse, equipped with comb, mirror, compact, etc.

Bad toys for trips:

1. Noise makers—the din is nerve-wracking and bothers the driver.

2. Small toys, like marbles, which get lost and frustrate the child.

3. Crayons, unless your child is very well co-ordinated. It is hard to color while moving, and crayons break and get lost.

4. Balloons—they want to hold them out windows, they hit the driver, and they pop.

5. Any toy that makes a good weapon in a fight.

Car rules:

It is wise to brief them on rules early, perhaps even the night before the trip. Then repeat, when you start.

1. No leaning against driver.

2. No beating driver on head.

3. No fooling with dashboard, if they sit in front.

4. No throwing things out windows.

5. No screaming, "Hello, dumb lady," to passersby.

Eating en route:

If the weather is good, picnic lunches are an excellent way of working off energy. Children can stretch their legs, and get a sense of freedom, before getting back into car.

Stopping to eat near a school playground is highly recommended.

You can have your car oiled and greased while you are eating in a restaurant or a nearby park.

The mother can go into the restaurant and find a table and order the meals while the father walks the children. This shortens the time the children have to sit still at a table, and saves the nerves of parents, waitresses and other guests. You can pay the bill the same way, too.

Don't be embarrassed to feed two small children on one adult order. Restaurants expect it. Often this is a better choice than the child's plate.

Many restaurants have Children's Service, which usually consists of silverware, napkin, plate, milk, and perhaps dessert. Then you feed them off your plate.

Be sure they have some food to start on right away, such as raw carrots or crackers.

Try to avoid restaurants during the rush hours.

Bedtime en route:

You might ask about a good place to spend the night while you are at the restaurant, and then phone ahead for reservations.

You can get your children toileted and into their sleepers after the evening meal, then drive on in the dark. The rhythm of the car will probably put them to sleep. When you stop at the motel, you can carry the bodies in.

Avoid heavy city traffic by getting up early in the morning.

You can make a child's bed out of an adult bed by pushing it against a wall, and lining the other side with the backs of chairs.

You can let your child "play house" in the motel for a few moments after arriving, allowing him to move chairs about and arrange things cozily. This may help him to feel at home—and he will go to sleep happily.

A way to make formula while driving:

1. Buy an electric sterilizer.

2. Wash bottles at night in hotel.

3. Fill each bottle with amount of water used in formula.

4. Put nipples on, nipples down.

5. Don't screw cap on too tightly. Leave room for steam expansion.

6. Put bottles in sterilizer and sterilize them. The water sterilizes with the bottles.

7. Fill one bottle with proper amount of canned milk. (Buy little cans, so you can throw them away.)

8. Add sugar or Karo or whatever you add.

9. Warm bottle on electric bottle warmer that plugs into cigarette lighter in car, or warm bottle in restaurant.

Trains:

Get a seat as near as possible to the rest rooms, water cooler and diner.

Planes:

It is a good idea to brief them in detail, because of the strange noises, and strange lights, and strange sensations. "We will get on the plane, and the lady will show us to our seats, and we will strap ourselves in, and then the motors will start to warm up—". And you might mention that there may be a funny feeling in their ears for a little while.

Don't rely on what the travel folders say. Take along some snacks yourself. And a blanket is useful, too.

Games for traveling:

1. "I see a horse," "I see a cow."

2. What kind of noises do cows make? And donkeys and diesel engines and ferry boats and babies and thunder and rain?

3. How many different kinds of machinery do you see?

4. Make wishes on first star, loads of hay, red-headed ladies, white horses, and cars with one light.

5. Songs: "The Bear Went Over the Mountain," "Come, Come, Come, Come to the Church in the Wildwood," "Old MacDonald Had a Farm," etc.

6. Opposites, for children four to five. What are the opposite words for dark, sad, fast, etc.?

CAN YOU GO CAMPING WITH CHILDREN?

Snuggle down in your sleeping bag
Underneath the moon,
And listen to the banjo
Play a goodnight tune.

—Margo Botsford

CAN YOU GO CAMPING WITH CHILDREN?

How old does a child have to be before you can take him camping? We might say it depends on the child. But it also depends on the parents. If the parents are devout campers themselves, they will go and take even baby. We have heard of a six-month-old infant who traveled through the wilds in a basket fashioned as a kayak attached to a burro's pack saddle. We have heard of a baby carried papoose-style, on a child's car seat mounted on a rucksack frame. But this is for those who are old camping enthusiasts. They will find a way, no matter what the obstacles are.

But for those parents who think camping might be nice but are timid about taking children along, for those who think it would be a cheap and pleasant vacation but feel insecure away from civilization with preschoolers—here are a few general rules we have learned from those who have tried it already, and who are planning to go again.

Prepare your child, in the same way we mentioned under Traveling. There will be two main changes in his routine, if you are really camping out under the stars. He will sleep out of doors, in a sleeping bag, and he won't have a bathroom. You can let him try out the sleeping bag at nap time in the backyard, if you want to. And if he has never used anything but a toilet since he was trained, you might let him be less inhibited on a picnic or Sunday drive. If he is used to his toilet seat, be sure to take it along.

What to take:

1. Mosquito netting is better than mosquito repellent, which children are apt to rub in their eyes.

2. First-aid kit, and snake-bite kit.

3. A harness with a leash is useful if you will be hiking on the brink of a canyon or swift stream.

4. For emotional needs—their favorite blanket or cuddly.

5. Frequent high-protein snacks are a good idea for high altitude appetites.

6. Sun equipment—sun hats and sunburn ointment.

7. Poison-oak remedies.

8. If you dress children in bright colors, they can be more easily seen from a distance.

9. Flashlights to take to bed in sleeping bags are often comforting.

Where to go:

If you are not too experienced, go to a good camp ground the first time. State or National Parks are equipped with tables, drinking water, toilets, fireplaces, sometimes even laundry rooms and showers.

You can write to the following addresses for information:

1. National Park Service, Department of Interior, Washington, D. C.

2. National Park Service, Department of Mines and Resources, Ottawa, Canada

3. Department of Agriculture, for a free booklet, entitled, "National Forest Vacations."

4. Sierra Club, 2061 Center Street, Berkeley 4, California

It is wise not to start off on a holiday weekend without making sure you can find a camp site at a crowded park.

If you are on a pack trip, it is a good idea to change camps in the mornings and eat lunch at the new camp site, which can be followed by a rest. Sometimes mothers and children go ahead, while fathers move camp.

Try to avoid poisonous-snake country. And check with your doctor on precautions to take if you are going into spotted-fever tick country.

If there are enough adults on a camping trip, some adults can take side trips, while the other adults stay with the children at camp.

Teach children what to do if they get lost. Stay still. Don't wander.

Things that are fun to do:
1. Singing and telling stories around the campfire.

2. Making dolls out of pine cones. Stick seeds or pebbles in the cones for eyes and noses. Wrap a bandana around it for a gown.

3. Children love to help wash clothes in a brook or pan, then spread them out flat on a hot rock to dry.

4. Gathering dirt or sand in a flat pan and arranging collections of tiny pine cones, twigs, shells or rocks.

5. Damming a shallow stream.

6. Making a wigwam out of a few sticks, an old blanket or tarp, and safety pins.

7. Making a swing or hammock between two trees out of extra rope and blankets.

And here is one mother's particular advice to new campers:

Our Camping Trip

If you like your comforts, find out which vacation spots have camp grounds maintained by the state, and you are likely to find a cleaner, more convenient place to stay. They usually have clean bathrooms, showers, and laundry tubs.

Plan your trip so you arrive at your camping site in the daylight. It also helps to get there at some hour when the children are not usually being fed or napped.

The idea of letting your child pack his favorite toys ahead of time is fine, if you can get across the idea of small, packable toys. The time to be firm is when leaving, not after you have trudged five miles through the forest lugging Junior's favorite dump truck. We took large plastic beach balls that were constantly blowing into ten feet of water, amid accompanying wails. And remember that you'll have to have room for some treasures coming home.

You will have to balance aesthetic advantages against practical ones in deciding how far to camp from the bathroom.

Sooner or later you will be faced with the problem of fending off little people while cooking a meal on the low, open stoves provided in state parks. They like to "help build the fire" with great quantities of hard-grained firewood and non-burning debris. We tried to provide certain times, one being before bedtime, when the cooking and washing chores are over and the fire is purely for enjoyment. Then they can poke at the fire while we watch, learning by experience what the dangers are, and satisfying their natural curiosity about fire. They will then accept the fact that the space in front of the fireplace is "No-Man's-Land" when meals are being prepared.

NATURE AND SCIENCE

Spring is showery, flowery, bowery;
Summer: hoppy, croppy, poppy;
Autumn: wheezy, sneezy, freezy;
Winter: slippy, drippy, nippy.

—Mother Goose

A child learns through his senses by watching, listening, tasting, smelling and touching. These direct experiences are stored away for now, but will serve as touchstones to new knowledge later on.

NATURE AND SCIENCE

The world, to a child, is like a foreign land is to us—filled with strange sights and curiosities. To explain the New, in context with the Familiar, is often a hard task for an adult. It's easier and more fun to have firsthand experience with nature and science in experiments and exploring.

You don't need to go far away to discover unexplored territory. A vacant lot is a jungle; a gutter, after the rain, is a fascinating body of water. Strange creatures hide under pieces of broken sidewalk, and you can usually find a spider web even in the tidiest of houses.

If you are going exploring, tie a big handkerchief with a snack in it on the child's belt. This way, he will have both hands free, and can later use this handkerchief to bring home the treasures. Coffee cans, paper bags and cardboard boxes also hold treasures. He may bring home leaves, cones, rocks, bugs and wild flowers; or he may bring rusty bolts, a piece of an old tire, a shoe, or a chunk of cement.

Special Excursions

Special excursions may be spontaneous, or well-planned adventures.

The firehouse: If your child is particularly interested in fire engines and playing fireman, he will appreciate the trip to the fire station. Most firemen are used to small children and will let them sit in the engine, try on their hats, and sound the siren.

A farm: A trip to a small farm where there are a few of the many kinds of farm animals is wonderful. You can see a farmer milk his cow at 5:30 or 6 in the evening, or 5:30 or 6 in the morning, if you get up early.

A train trip: A short train trip on a local train is very exciting, and children under five get to ride free!

Watching a new house grow: Bulldozing, laying bricks, pouring cement, hammering and pounding—all have a fascination for a child, particularly when what is being built is something as familiar as a house. If it is a wood house, you can talk about that. "First we grow the tree, then when it is very old we cut it down, send it to the lumber mill, etc."

A pet shop: Most pet shop owners are patient people who understand children and animals. A good shop to visit would be one that has a variety of monkeys, parrots and wild birds, and small animals. Seeing these animals and birds at close range is often better for small children than a trip to the zoo.

The five-minute car wash: It is much more exciting if you get to ride through the system inside the car instead of watching from the outside. The washing and drying has such force that it is like being in a violent storm.

Machinery: Automobile and farm-machinery show rooms or factories where a familiar product is made, such as ice cream or candy, are of particular interest.

Workmen at your house: Draw a chalk line on the floor or a string across the door, and let the child watch the plumber or paper hanger from this "spectator's box."

Children love to drive by the old house where you used to live, or see the church where you got married, or the hospital where they were born, or the school you used to go to, or the school they will go to when they are old enough.

And they like to go up on the roof with Daddy when he adjusts the antenna or cleans out the drain pipe, and they can yell at people down on the sidewalk and yell down the chimney. Roof Day isn't a very good activity for the roof and isn't too safe for children; it depends a lot on the roof, the daddy, and the child. Climbing up steep stairs into the attic can be Attic Day and down steep stairs into the cellar, Cellar Day. Places where you go only occasionally, and only if you must be very careful, are big events for children.

The Weather

Weather is just as important to a child as it is to an adult.

Rain: When a child has to stay indoors on a rainy day, it helps to explain why it rains and why we need rain. In explaining, start with clouds. Clouds are hundreds and hundreds of raindrops in the air. When clouds get too heavy to float in the air, they fall down and that is rain. The sun is still up in the sky and is still shining, but we can't see it.

Sit by the window and watch the raindrops race each other down the pane. And when the rain is over, put on rain clothes and splash in puddles, sail boats in gutters, and watch for the rainbow.

See how bright and clean the garden looks after rain. And how fresh it smells.

See how much water is in the tin can you put out before the rain started to fall.

(See Things To Do and Making Things.)

Wind: Wind is air going fast. Without air, we couldn't breathe, birds couldn't fly. Without wind we couldn't fly kites or watch the trees bend. And the wind bell wouldn't tinkle. (See Things To Save for wind bell making.)

Wet your finger and hold it up in the air to see which way the wind is blowing.

Snow: Snow is the same as rain coming down. Only the air is colder and the raindrops turn to snowflakes. Snow is the time for snowmen and snow houses and snow balls. And for making angels in the snow bank by lying flat on your back and moving your arms from above your head down to your sides.

Bring some snow inside and watch it melt, or make snow ice cream by adding a few drops of vanilla and a little sugar to clean snow.

Snow is the time to feed the birds. Birds like bread crumbs, cracker crumbs, seeds, popcorn, peanut butter, cranberries, and fat from meat. A window sill will attract some birds, or a feeding tray can be located around your yard so you can watch them eat. Make a suet stick by drilling holes in a branch and stuffing it with fat, or stock food or fat in a big pine cone and hang it from a branch of a tree. Hang the branch or cone low enough so you can refill it easily.

A child will learn that, if he is very quiet, he can sit on one end of a park bench and birds will eat the food he has provided on the other end of the bench.

The World and The Universe

When children begin to invent explanations of the universe, the time has come to help them understand some facts established by

131

science. Even if you know a lot about planets, stars, constellations and eclipses, keep it to yourself or limit it to naming Venus and a few simple facts such as these.

The globe is the easiest way to explain why, when it is night for us, the sun is shining on the children of China and they are eating their lunch. If you don't have a globe, use a grapefruit for the sun, and an orange for the earth. Holding the grapefruit steady, slowly move the orange or the globe to show how the world moves slowly, revolving around the sun.

Sun: The sun is always shining brightly, even if we can't see it. The sun is so hot we cannot look at it. It has to be hot to keep us warm and help plants to grow.

In the daytime when the sun is shining, you can see your shadow. A shadow is a place where, for the moment, the light cannot shine. Sometimes your shadow is tall and skinny (when it is behind you), and sometimes it is short and fat (when the sun is above you). The sun is so far away that no one can ever go there.

Moon: But someday, maybe, someone will go to the moon in a rocket ship because it is not so far away. The moon looks round and full like a great canteloupe only once a month. Then it begins to look smaller and smaller until it is like only a slice of canteloupe. But all the moon is still there; we can see only part of it because earth is casting its shadow on it.

Stars: The moon looks bigger than the stars, but the stars are really much bigger. And it is because they are farther away that they look smaller. Stars are in the sky all the time, only you can't see them because the sun is so bright.

Watch for the first star of the evening. Teach children "Star Light, Star Bright, First Star I've Seen Tonight...." or "Twinkle, Twinkle...."

Watch for a "falling" star. If you can say "money, money, money," very fast before it is through falling, you will eventually become rich.

On hot summer nights, it is fun to lie on your back in the yard and look and look at the stars.

Clouds: It is fun to watch clouds in the daytime which sometimes look like Easter bunnies, bears, people's faces, cotton candy, or whatever else you might imagine.

Time and Space

Clocks: What is important on a clock is to know when it is time for juice and crackers, when it is time for naps, and when it is

132

time for Daddy to come home. Draw a clock face from a paper plate (as described in the section Making Things) to help show the different times.

Calendars: What is important to know on a calendar is the date of your birthday and the day it comes, when Christmas comes, or when vacation time comes.

You can circle these days and count them off when time is getting short by X-ing them out or using pins or map tacks. Each day, move the pin over one more space. Make a calendar for the week or the month and hang it in a prominent spot so significant days can be noted. "Tuesday is the day you go to the doctor's, Thursday is a birthday party, Saturday you get a nickel to spend any way you want, and on Sunday, Daddy stays home."

Maps: What is important to know on a map is where your house is, or where Grandma lives, or where you went on your vacation. You can draw a simple map of your neighborhood and put in the store and the path across the field, and the houses of everyone who is your friend.

Compass: A compass is magic. No matter which way you turn it, it always points the same direction.

Magnet: A magnet is a force which will pick up a bobby pin, but will not pick up a toothpick. Playing with magnets is more fun than trying to explain why they do what they do.

Speed: What is important about airplanes is that they go so fast. Much faster than trains or buses. If you go to Grandmother's house on an airplane, it only takes six hours; if you go on the train, it takes two days and one night; if you drive in a car, it takes five days; if you go on horses, it takes weeks; and if you walk, you'll never make it.

Growth: You know your hair is growing because you have to get haircuts, and your finger nails are growing because they need to be clipped. But you can't see yourself grow!

A "Birthday Board" is a place where you stand still every year, and someone makes a mark on the board at the top of your head and writes your name and the date next to it. Photographs help prove that Mother was once a little girl, rode a bike, graduated from high school, and got married. Bringing the album up to date shows Mother carrying the child in her stomach, home from the hospital, and with baby's first birthday cake. This gives the child the feeling of the rhythm of life and a sense of the spaciousness of time.

133

Pretending electricity isn't invented yet:

> Everything wasn't always the way it is now. When Grandpa was a boy, there weren't any airplanes or telephones or electricity. You can pretend you are Grandpa, long ago. You can turn out all the lights, then light a candle and sit around it and talk. You can talk about the shadows, the dark, and the way the candle burns. You can give each child a piece of wax to play with. This is a cozy, relaxing experience, because you can't do anything else, like washing dishes or listening to TV (TV is electric).

Natural Surroundings

Birds: Just as you put a feeding tray and a suet branch out for the birds in the winter, (see preceding section) you can also put out for them in the spring materials which birds can use to build their nests. Put yarn, string, or torn rags on a branch.

Worms: In the gutter after rain, one may find angleworms to transplant to the back-yard garden. Explain to the child who thinks you are burying animals alive that angleworms live in the soil and work the soil like a cultivator or plow.

Collections: Children of preschool age collect rocks, shells, leaves, cones, and berries with very little aesthetic discrimination. They are mostly interested in "lots." Nor are they very interested in display. Just shoe boxes full are satisfying to them.

> Rocks and shells can be used in the turtle bowl or fish bowl, or in bottles where plants grow in water.
> Big rocks can be doorstops.
> Smaller rocks can be paperweights.
> Little shells that have a hole in them can be strung into a necklace.

> Four-year-olds can draw around leaves and then color their drawings.

> Pressing leaves in a book is fun because you usually forget about them and then when you remember them, they are nice and flat. Then you can mount them on colored paper and hang them on the wall.

> Pine cones are pretty just as they are. But they are also pretty when painted, and children like to paint pine cones and acorns for decorations. They often enjoy sending some to Grandmother, who usually reports it was her favorite gift.

Growing Things Outdoors

It has been said that children who help plant gardens from the beginning never walk on plants, but cut bouquets for the table with long stems.

A child may be very enthusiastic about putting the seeds in the ground and watering them for a time. But even the growth of radishes is too slow for him to remember his garden and the duties connected with gardening for very long. You probably wouldn't want him in there with a hoe anyway, so consider planting and watering his activity, and weeding and cultivating yours.

Caster beans, sunflower seeds, and string beans produce tremendous rewards because of their giant size and rapid growth. The child also gets a great sense of accomplishment from growing corn, pumpkins, radishes, or a favorite vegetable. And with flowers, the old hardies such as zinnias, marigolds, nasturtiums, and bulbs are sure to grow and bloom with minimum attention.

Plants that are going to be transplanted later can be started in cardboard milk cartons. Rip the carton down to size and then when you are ready to transplant, it is easy to peel off the rest of the cardboard without disturbing the roots.

Smaller plants can be started in halves of eggshells. While they are growing it is better to keep them in the egg carton; but a single shell can be supported with a piece of modeling clay.

Use a popsicle stick or wooden ice-cream spoon for a garden marker, and use indelible ink to label your varieties.

Growing Things Indoors

A narcissus bulb will grow in a shallow bowl with water and a few pebbles or shells to support the bulb. Keep a ruler handy and measure the growth each day. Everyone will be surprised.

A sweet potato can be sprouted in a glass of water by putting the narrow end half down into the water. Toothpicks can support it. The roots will grow first, and then the vine will start to grow if you remember to add water occasionally and keep it in a sunny place.

Carrots will grow lovely new fern if you will cut off the top of the carrot and cut away most of the old fern, keeping the tops in water in a shallow bowl.

Avocado seeds will sprout by using much the same process as for sweet potatoes, only the results are not so fast nor so sure.

A piece of ivy or Wandering Jew will grow roots in water, and the cutting can later be potted.

Experiments With Plants

Pumpkin: One of the best experiments to show children the complete cycle of a living thing is to save the pumpkin seeds from the Halloween pumpkin and plant them in the spring. Put them in a dry place and spread them out so that they will not rot. Soaking them overnight the day before planting will help insure success. After the child has seen the vines grow and bloom and watched the green pumpkins turn orange, he is ready to select one for his jack-o-lantern, hollow the insides out, and save the seeds to plant in the spring all over again.

Grass: An indoor experiment that is fun to watch is growing grass seed or bird seed on a sponge that is kept very wet and given plenty of sunlight. Keep the sponge in a saucer of water.

Dry beans: Lima beans or navy beans will swell the first day they are put in water, and the next day or two the bean will open and start to sprout. Keeping the bean on a piece of wet cotton will prevent it from drying out. It must not be completely submerged, because it needs air too.

Experiments With Food in the Kitchen

Bread: Yeast makes gases and the gas makes the dough get bigger and bigger.

Bread that is left uncovered gets dry.

Bread that is covered too long gets mold on it.

Melting: Butter melts if you leave it out on a hot day. Butter melts if you heat it in a saucepan on the stove. Ice melts and ice cream melts. It is better to have ice cream melt in your mouth unless you prefer "soup ice cream."

Whipping: Potatoes that are cooked and beaten are called mashed potatoes. Egg whites that are whipped are called meringue when it's on top of a pie, and whipped cream that is whipped too long is called butter. It you make butter this way, (probably by accident) add salt to the whipped cream. But your children won't believe it's butter until you add a few drops of yellow food coloring.

Pets

Anything that lives can be a pet. It all depends upon your tastes and your psychological background. If you are squeamish about hamsters and white mice for pets, you will almost certainly transfer this fear to your child. If your child has a fancy for worms and you can't stand them, encourage caterpillars or lightning bugs.

Many small creatures such as butterflies or lizards are happier in their own homes, which are not inside bottles.

Insects: Don't underestimate insects as pets for small children. Insects breathe, hear, see, smell, taste, and feel. They don't take up nearly as much room as a German Shepherd. And they eat less. Just add a new green leaf every day. Part of a nylon stocking stretched tight over the jar and held with a rubber band gives them more air than a few holes poked in the top. It's good to know the names of some good insects like lady bug, and the bad ones like aphis and mosquitoes. (Lady bugs eat aphis.)

Angleworms: Angleworms can be kept in a box of soil and each worm given a name and treated like a friend.

Caterpillars: A caterpillar that has formed a web around itself can be found on leaves of bushes and trees. This cocoon can be kept inside a jar with air holes, and a butterfly should emerge.

Fish: Guppies are good for small children because they carry their eggs in their stomach and give birth to real live fish. Most goldfish in a bowl are not terribly fascinating, even when you find out that fish have ears buried in their heads, and noses, not to breathe through, but to smell through. They breathe through their gills.

Turtles: The little dime-store turtle is fine, but the bigger box turtle is more fun. He doesn't live in water and can stay in a carton or the whole back yard if he is fenced. He likes raw meat and lettuce leaves.

Fowl: It's hard to make a pet out of a chicken, but a duck will let you hold him, and he will follw you. Girl ducks lay eggs (in a nest) that are good to eat. A duck in the garden will eat all the snails as well as the bugs. But they are also vegetarians and like primroses, too. If you take the quack out of a duck because the neighbors complain, you must be prepared to watch over him for life, as he cannot protect himself. The same is true of descenting a skunk and we will mention it here, as we do not plan a special section on skunks as pets.

Frogs: A frog starts his life as an egg and inside the egg is an embryo. The embryo hatches into a tadpole and at this point your child's experience with it will probably begin. In a few weeks he gets two back legs and two front legs and now he is a pollywog. When his tail disappears he is a frog, and frogs can jump and get away from you, so don't let him out of your sight or you won't have him for long.

Birds: Parakeets or budgies have taken the country by storm in the last few years. Two parakeets in a cage will talk to each other and are not so likely to talk to you. Even if parakeets don't talk, they are pretty, easy to care for, and will sit on the child's shoulder or finger. They need to be let out of their cage every day to exercise their wings. They live to an old age if windows are closed and the cats are outside.

Cats: These long-suffering animals are very good with small children, provided they have both grown up knowing each other when each was small. They are willing to play "Baby" and will line up with the Teddy bears on the beds at night. Something that purrs when you hug it seems to give special comfort. A very good experience for the child is to see her mother cat have babies.

Dogs: No two people could ever agree on the type of dog for small children. But generally, it's a good idea that if the child is very small, the dog should be pretty big in order to take care of itself.

A good place for a puppy is in an old play pen. Tear open cardboard boxes and line the sides of the pen so he can't get out.

If the puppy gets lonesome at night, the sound of a clock ticking close to him offers comfort.

Or if he seems cold, a bottle of warm water with a tight lid can be placed in his box.

Two or three jingle bells sewed tight in a piece of cloth is a good toy for a puppy, and pacifiers are fun for him to chew on.

MONEY

I had a penny, a bright, new penny,
I took my penny to the market square.

—When We Were Very Young
A. A. Milne

MONEY

(As your child will probably attach the same value to
money as you do, we won't go into much theory here.)

A child's first impression of money is that it is something grownups like, so he does, too. He notices that it has a nice shape, and a pleasant, hard feel, and makes a good noise when it jingles.

But the moment he tries to get hold of some of it, he is told two facts: Money is not something to put into your mouth, even though it feels nice there. And, second, money is not to play with!

By the time he is around three he learns that money has another value—it can buy nice things, like balls, gum, or balloons. But when he asks for it, he is apt to be told that if he is old enough to spend it, he is old enough to earn it—which is not true; or, he is not old enough for an allowance—which is not true either.

Soon after this he finds out that some kids are "rich" and some kids are "poor," and it is better to be "rich" than "poor."

So you can see your money troubles start at preschool age.

Here are a few ways preschoolers can learn to handle money and also have fun:

A pig bank for relatives to put money in. It is amazing how much of a treat it is just to drop a penny in a pig bank, accompanied by much ceremony.

When he is old enough, let him run into a store with some money for a simple purchase. It doesn't take very long, either, for him to learn to return the change to you.

Money teaches people to make choices, which is a mature thing to learn. Let him have a nickel that will buy an ice-cream cone or a plastic car, and let him decide which, if it is not too difficult for him.

Give him play money. A toy wallet is fun, too. You can play Store with him, and around four and a half, you can even play Savings Bank.

Tell him how Daddy earns the money, and how it is used. Let him visit Daddy at work, if possible.

Let him in on simple, not-too-long-range decisions you are making, such as saving for a TV set, or power lawn mower.

Let him have five cents a week, and give it to him, even when he forgets to ask for it. He can spend it when you go to the grocery store, and this will also prevent nagging for everything in sight.

Don't start a work program to earn money until you think he is ready for it. Most children, at preschool age, are too young to carry through.

Don't pay him for ordinary household jobs which will eventually be part of his responsibility anyway. Otherwise he will begin to bargain for money every time he ties his own shoes.

Don't take an allowance away for bad behavior. What if your husband took away your household money every time he disagreed with you about something? An allowance has to be a certain amount of money which can be counted on, every week.

Don't let him handle amounts of money that will upset you if he loses it.

At Christmas time, let your child have ten or twenty or one hundred pennies. Show him how he can divide them up to buy gifts for everyone.

If your child is given money, offer to keep it in a special place, just for him.

When he goes to the bank with you, explain that this is where you keep your money, just like his pig bank.

Be sure the principles you learned about money as a child are still valid in present-day society before you pass them on as Absolute Standards. Credit, for example, used not to be so respectable. And a nickel doesn't go as far as it used to. Taking a little child into a dime store to spend a nickel may be a frustrating experience.

Things Children Sometimes Do With Money:

Spend it foolishly. (A Best Buy to you is not necessarily a Best Buy to them.)

Bribe other children.

Give it away.

Lose it.

Hoard it.

You can guide them with your best advice, but remember that just having the use of some money is good experience.

SITTERS

Everything was just fine, Mrs. Brown,
until you came home.

—What Sitters Say

SITTERS

Sometimes you have to be away, and sometimes you just want to be away for a while. This is when sitters are necessary.

Most of you know the obvious ways of finding and using a sitter, but we have also included some different and useful suggestions.

It is a good idea to find a sitter and try her out before you have to have one for an important occasion. In fact, you might try to get two or three on your string. You will then avoid that Trapped Feeling.

Some mothers like to stay at home the first time they use a new sitter. This will depend on your children, however, for many children won't go near a sitter until the mother leaves.

If you have moved into a new neighborhood, ask a neighbor if she knows of a good sitter. (Don't be a Sitter Stealer, however.) You can also take your children for a walk, and explore for sitters. Find an older lady, or a high-school girl, check on her with a neighbor, and then ask her if she will Sit for you.

One of the nicest things about finding a sitter who lives nearby, or who drives her own car, is that you will avoid that long drive to her home late at night.

Call the nearest high school or college, which usually have sitter listings. One family we know had an Indian prince, an exchange student, for a sitter, until his father died and he had to go home and rule his country. After that they had to convince the children that all sitters did not wear turbans.

There may be a sitter service in your community. If it is a reliable service, it usually requires its members to have blood tests and chest X-rays. However, they are often more expensive and insist on minimum hours. If their minimum is four hours, and you are only going out for two hours, you may feel a little depressed about the waste of money. It is also difficult to get the same sitter over and over, particularly if she is a good one.

Some young mothers find it easier to direct a younger girl. Older ladies, though often excellent sitters, sometimes are set in their ways and may be shocked to learn that your two-year-old is not yet toilet trained, or that little boys do not always stay clean. It is nice, however, for children to know members of the older generation, especially if their grandparents live far away.

Many mothers have discovered the value of an older boy, especially if they have boy children. Boy sitters will play baseball or tell fishing stories to impressionable little boys, which is a very special treat.

If there is a nine, ten or eleven-year-old in your neighborhood who would enjoy making a small amount of money, you may find him useful as a sitter while you stay home to bake a cake or write letters. He can play with the children, or take them for a walk, and you are near if needed.

If your child is just starting to go outside the gate to play, you can hire a twelve-year-old to watch him during the first transition weeks, until you feel certain of his traffic habits. This gives the child a sense of freedom without the danger.

Some parents hire a sitter to read or play with the children in their room while they give a party. If the sitter is a familiar friend, some children enjoy spending the night at her house.

Other mothers hire high-school girls to come in after school a regular number of days a week, to give the children supper and a bath. In this way they can count on certain times to make appointments, shop or just rest.

You cannot expect a sitter to do dishes and other housework without arranging this with her ahead of time, and paying her accordingly.

Another mother who had a series of doctor appointments, and who did not want to have to pay for a regular sitter so often for such a short time, hired a twelve-year-old girl to drive downtown with her and her small children. Then she dropped the children and the sitter at a playground nearby, while she went to the doctor's office. This cost her twenty-five cents instead of one to three dollars.

You can hire a young girl sitter to come in every Saturday, so you can be free to play golf or shop.

Summertime is an excellent time to get high-school girls, other than weekends.

It sometimes makes a vacation more fun for adults to take a sitter along. You must be careful not to overburden her, however, and to see that she also enjoys herself. It is a good idea to plan the trip with her before hand. You might arrange that you will watch the children on the beach every afternoon, if you can have your evenings free.

How To Organize Your Own Sitter Club:

If you go out regularly, sitters can be expensive. Also, in many of the new surburban housing tracts there is a majority of young parents of the same age, and very few high-school children or older ladies. In this case it is convenient to trade off with other mothers, or to organize your own "sitter club."

Setting up a sitter club requires an occasional meeting to write up the rules.

In one typical, successful sitter club, the rules are as follows:

1. One mother acts as secretary each month.

2. Membership is limited to twenty couples, and new members have to be recommended by old members.

3. The number of hours any one couple can be ahead or behind is fifteen. Some couples lead a more active social life than others, and it seems unfair to let some get further ahead in hours that they will never use up in a year, or other couples so far behind that they will never catch up.

4. Each member is required to use the club—either to sit or be sat for—at least once every three months, just to stay active.

5. As the heaviest demand for sitting is on Saturday night, everyone is required to take that night at least once a month, if called upon.

6. To arrange a sit, members call the secretary who keeps a ledger with all the names and number of hours each couple is ahead or behind. She tries to arrange sits first for those couples who are furthest in debt.

7. Sits cannot begin before seven, unless you make your own personal arrangement.

8. Children are to be fed and dressed in their night clothes on the arrival of the sitter, though they may still be up.

9. No one is asked to sit with a sick child.

10. Double time is given when children of more than one family are being cared for in one sit.

11. Leave some coffee on the stove and a pillow and blanket on the sofa for the sitter's comfort.

Many fathers like to take the sits because other people's children are often better about going to bed for them, and they can finish the work they brought home from the office.

It is also a natural, friendly atmosphere in which children already know the sitters and the sitter's children. Sometimes the sitter's whole family will come over early in the evening with a watermelon or ice cream, and stay until it is time for all the children to go to bed. You can go out, knowing that your children will feel at home with the sitter.

Lists To Leave for Sitters:

It is always a good idea to leave certain phone numbers and directions, outside of the particular instructions you may give your sitter. If you are going out for the evening, the following phone numbers are appreciated by the sitter:

1. Close neighbor with car

2. Children's doctor

3. The number where you will be, if possible

4. Fire

5. Police

Tell the sitter if your child has any special habit, such as taking a Cuddly or a chewing blanket to bed, or leaving the light on or the door open. Show the sitter how to work the radio and the heat.

If you are going out of town for a weekend or longer, it is a good idea to leave a drug-store and grocery-store phone number where the sitter can charge. You might also leave her some extra money for an emergency.

If your sitter comes fifteen minutes to a half hour ahead of the time you leave, it will ease the transition, give you a chance to watch the sitter in action, give you time to remember last-minute instructions, and perhaps give you some time to dress.

Many children behave better with a sitter than with their parents, and that is another reason why it is a good idea to have a sitter now and then. It gives your children practice in being especially nice.

A number of people are happy we have finished this book. Those especially happy are David, Jimmy, Elizabeth, Nick and Mike.

David is waiting to make a map of his neighborhood, showing where Ricky, Bobby and Danny live.

Jimmy wants to make a Woo Woo.

Elizabeth wants to hammer two pieces of wood together and make a sign that says KEEP OFF for her yard.

Nick and Mike want to make a "Billy Book" for their friend, Margit Hind, who is having her tonsils out next week.

So that is what we are going to do now.

WE SHOULD LIKE TO THANK THE MANY PARENTS (AND A FEW WHO AREN'T PARENTS) WHO HAVE HELPED US WRITE THIS BOOK. IN PARTICULAR:

Addie Axelrod
Joe Axelrod
Pat Gillespie
Lucille West
Dorothy Johnson
Mary Margaret Boyd
Eloise McMurtry
Katie Dalton
Carolyn MacKinnon

Mary Elizabeth Van Patten
Cecilie Scoggins
Lydia Verbarg
Margery Gray
Flossy Rowlands
Rose Evans
Randy Zulch
Rosemary Jones
Muriel Romelfanger

Medrith Appling
Alice Wegg
Ardyce Stein
Clyde Miller
Jean McDowell
Janice Hittenberger
Gunvar Sweetman
Hanne Lore Nepote
Anne Foote
Virginia Baker
Doris Quarg
Mary Hood
Doris Denhart
Bobby Browne
Margaret Muser
Virginia Griffin
Clara Mae Wenborn
Eileen Jones
Martha Ziegler
Betsy Fiksdahl
Joyce Fisher
Joan Warmbrunn
Jane Henderson
Florence LaRiviere
Afton Ward
Virginia Boone
Ruth Douglas
Pat Shinn
Ruth Lay
Sylvia Hoyt

Sally Faulkner
Joan Donegan
Margo Meblin
Margo Botsford
Rennie Wilsnack
Phyllis Hind
Hilda Krech
Barbara Gilman
Jean Van Pelt
Midge Stein
Lois Wadsworth
Mary Ellen Dornbush
Marianne Crowder
Mildred Davis
Penny Dawson
Betty Garbett
Mary Lee Valentine
Marilyn Blackhurst
Marge Childreth
Elizabeth Dana
Marcia Jacoby
Ann Hamill
Peggy Howell
Mildred Mendelowitz
Dorothea Bamford
Jane Muheim
Ann Scowcroft
Polly Cooperrider
Barbara Kline
Carol Hardgrove